PLEASE, GOD, HELP!

Please, God, Help!

*I have cried out to you, Yahweh, from your holy presence.
You send me a Father's help.*
—Psalm 3:4

Virginia Dawkins

XULON PRESS

Xulon Press
2301 Lucien Way #415
Maitland, FL 32751
407.339.4217
www.xulonpress.com

© 2020 by Virginia Dawkins

All rights reserved solely by the author. The author guarantees all contents are original and do not infringe upon the legal rights of any other person or work. No part of this book may be reproduced in any form without the permission of the author. The views expressed in this book are not necessarily those of the publisher.

Unless otherwise indicated, Scripture quotations taken from the New King James Version (NKJV). Copyright © 1982 by Thomas Nelson, Inc. Used by permission. All rights reserved.

Printed in the United States of America.

ISBN-13: 978-1-6305-0748-0

Introduction

There is a connection between Earth and Heaven, a passageway that leads straight to the throne of the Heavenly Father. We cry out, and our pleas travel into the heavens. John tells us in Revelation that our Father welcomes our prayers as "sweet incense," and that He collects them upon the golden altar that is before the throne.

The first prayer I can remember praying was when I was five years old. It was a desperate, childish prayer when I looked out an open window one day and saw my daddy carrying a suitcase as he hurried toward the bus stop. I cried out to him, begging him to come back, but it was like my daddy did not hear. I began to call out to God: "Please, God, Help! Bring him back. Let my daddy come back home and live with us!"

I felt that God did not hear my pleas. For years after that, He seemed to be so far away, somewhere up there in the sky looking down, judging my sins. Later I walked down the aisle of the Baptist Church and prayed the Sinner's Prayer. I know that God heard and answered that prayer, but in my mind, He was still so far away, looking down with critical eyes.

I did not know then that God actually knew me, even before I was conceived, that He formed me in my mother's womb, that He loved me, even on my worst days, and that He had a good plan for my life. I did not know that just as God had desired to talk with Adam and Eve in the garden, He also wanted to talk with me each day.

As I read the Scriptures, I began to see the Jesus who walked this earth and experienced every temptation, every pain, every betrayal, and disconnect that we humans experience. I saw the relationship of the Father with His Son. There was a degree of separation between them while Jesus was walking as a man on earth. However, the Father provided a way, a divine connection between Himself and the Son, between heaven and earth: Prayer.

Time with the Father was a priority with Jesus:

> "So, He Himself often withdrew into the wilderness and prayed" (Luke 5:16).

> "And when He had sent the multitudes away, He went up on the mountain by Himself to pray. Now when evening came, He was alone there" (Matthew 14:23).

> "In the early morning, while it was still dark, Jesus got up, left the house, and went away to a secluded place and was praying there" (Mark 1:35).

> "He went out to the mountain to pray, and continued all night in prayer to God" (Luke 6:12).

To communicate with a Holy God—what an awesome privilege!

At the cross, Jesus offered Himself as the only fully sufficient sacrifice to pay the penalty for our sins. Because Jesus, through His death on the Cross, reconciled me with the Father. I can "draw near with confidence to the throne of grace and receive help in times of need." I am still the little girl who cries out to God, sometimes in fear, sometimes in faith, but now I know that He hears my every plea. I pray to a God who sometimes says no, but has often surprised me by doing abundantly above all I could ask or dream.

I pray to God in heaven, in the name of Jesus Christ my Savior. Yes, what an awesome privilege!

Table of Contents

1. These Things I Know To Be True 1
   Wake Up and Pray!
   Please, God, Help!
   Mother Knows Best
   On an Ordinary Day
   Building a Bridge to Heaven
   Asking
   Scary Places
   Ageless Spirit
   Uncle Nelson
   Prayers For Betty Jo

2. How To Pray 23
   The Model Prayer
   Rules For Prayer
   The Prince of Preachers
   Try Prayer Power
   Intercessory Prayer
   Break Through Prayer
   Patience
   George Muller's Prayers
   George Muller's Financial Advice
   The Name of Jesus
   The Circle Maker
   Pray Like Daniel

    The Prayer of Jabez
    The Man Who Asked Questions
    Debbie's Perfect Word
    Prayer Prescription
    Keeping Things Wound

3. Life Saving Prayers 47
    Jerry's Prayer
    Praying for Strangers
    Street Prayers
    The Choice
    Don't Ever Give Up!
    The Teacher Who Learned to Pray

4. Prayers That Never Die 57
    Monica's Prayers
    Sonya's Prayers
    Victor's Mother
    A Father's Prayers

5. Impossible Things 65
    Brooklyn Tabernacle Church
    Heaven Is For Real
    To Heaven And Back
    The Last Survivor of Nine Eleven
    God Wants to Do Impossible Things

6. Journaling 75
    Change Your Life
    Mark Batterson's Journal
    Flannery O'Connor's Journal
    The Diary of a Young Girl
    Journaling Feelings
    My Journal
    Inspiring Quotes From My Journal

7. Giving Thanks... 85
    Choosing to Give Thanks
    Saying Grace
    Pizza, Pasta, & Prayer

8. Praying For Our Nation 93
    The Remnant
    Shaping History Through Prayer
    The Hardest Thing
    What Does God Desire For America?

Notes 99

Chapter One

These Things I Know To Be True

Be careful not to forget the things you have seen God do for you. Keep reminding yourself and tell your children and your grandchildren too.
            —Deuteronomy 4:9

WAKE UP AND PRAY!

Prayer is the Holy Spirit finding a desire in the heart of the Father, putting it in your heart and sending it back to heaven in the power of the Cross.
            –Adrian Rogers

"Where is Tanzania?" Mary Jo woke me with a phone call, and my sleepy brain had no answer for her question. "I don't know," I said. "We can look it up on the map, but why do you ask so early in the morning?"

"It's not early for me. I've been awake since three o'clock this morning, with that one word on my brain—Tanzania. You know how that happens to me sometimes, just the one word. It didn't come from my natural brain; I can't even remember where that place is. I haven't read or heard anything about it lately—but I know Who woke me."

Mary Jo's heart is tuned and ready for responding to the "still, small voice" of God in the night hours as well as at unexpected times of the day. Often, God will put one word, or a person's name in her mind, and she knows she is to pray. So, my intercessor friend got out of bed, went to her knees and prayed for that far-away place, with no knowledge of what was going on there.

Later, while listening to the news on the radio, she heard that a train wreck had occurred in Tanzania at the time of her prayers. The next day we found a short article in the newspaper that more clearly explained:

TRAIN RIDE TURNS INTO A 25-MINUTE HORROR

"What started as a slow roll backward for a passenger train crossing Central Tanzania accelerated into a screaming, twenty-five minute runaway ride that ended when it crashed into a lumbering freight train... 174 bodies were pulled from the wreckage ... Survivors from the morning crash described how most of the 1,200 people on board were praying—some quietly, some loudly—while others screamed as the train swayed from side to side..."

We saw it so clearly then. When God hears his people crying out for help, He alerts others to pray in their behalf. God heard the frightened prayers of people on a runaway train in East Africa and woke someone on another continent to pray. Most likely, God woke others at the same time. Perhaps many lives were saved because people heard God's voice, just as Mary Jo did, and took part in a process of intercessory prayer.

Please, God, Help!

May the Lord answer you in the day of trouble; may the name of the God of Jacob defend you; may He send you help from the sanctuary.
  - Psalm 20:1

After his last swallow of beer in the airport grill, he flashed a boyish grin, walked up the ramp, and disappeared into the plane. I drove out of the parking lot while the airplane sailed into a blue sky, taking my little brother on a journey toward a jungle in Vietnam. Tears eased down my cheeks and plopped on the steering wheel as I craned my neck for one more glance at the shiny aircraft growing smaller, then becoming a dot in distant clouds.

Our soldier was young and unsettled. Was he ready to fight? Was he ready to die if that was his fate? Mom and I woke every morning with a prayer on our lips, "Please, God, take care of him. Let him come back home alive." We were not skilled in proper ways to pray. We couldn't list the requirements for answered prayer, nor had we memorized effective scriptures to quote. We knew that people died every day in Vietnam; we wondered why God would answer our prayers. But we prayed.

Months later, in a foxhole tunneled out in the midst of thick jungle brush, my brother crouched low, as the Viet Cong approached. He gripped his weapon and prepared to aim, but fear paralyzed him when he realized his gun was jammed. Trapped inside that hole of slimy water, filled with bugs, bullets zinged overhead, footsteps inched closer. His heart-beat throbbed in his ears and temples like loud drum-beats, while huge drops of sweat showered down on the useless gun. This was it; he was going to die! As his life passed before him, he remembered how Mama prayed on her knees beside the bed. From that image, my brother began to whisper: "God, please help!" as his words silently passed toward the heavens, a strange thing happened. An awesome presence came into the bunker, like a soft breeze, hovering over the foxhole, surrounding, hiding and protecting the young man. Fear disappeared and was replaced by perfect peace, as the enemy turned away.

Later on, a bullet ripped through my brother's rib-cage, barely missing his heart. A helicopter moved in and rescued him in the midst of enemy fire. After several months in the hospital, he recovered, went back into the jungle in the heat of battle, and survived once again.

Months later, we watched him step out of another airplane and walk toward us. The boyish grin had disappeared, replaced by the forced smile of a man who had witnessed too much pain and death. Nevertheless, he was alive because God heard our prayers.

Many times, we can only cry out a quick plea: "Please, God, Help!" But there are other times when we must stay on our knees in prolonged intercession. Prayers travel more speedily than bullets, prompting God to wrap airplanes in angel's wings. Prayers follow our loved ones across the ocean and into hostile countries. They weave through barbed-wire fences and penetrate steel gates. Prayers, even baby-like prayers, are the greatest power that we possess.

Mother Knows Best

Relying on God has to begin all over again every day as if nothing had yet been done.
—C.S. Lewis

When I was a toddler, just learning to talk, this is the first sentence I put together: "I not listening." According to Mom's story, I pulled away from her protective hand and ran ahead down the dusty road leading to the country store. When she ran after me and called, "Mary Virginia, come back and hold my hand," I discovered my newfound language skills and retorted, "I not listening!" I demonstrated a similar attitude in my teenage years, rebelling against Mom's old-fashioned rules. But Mom was persistent, and some of her instructions began shaping my life.

Maybe it was what I observed more than what I heard that made the greatest impact. Mom was on her knees a lot; she talked to God about everything. I decided there had to be a God, because she spent so much time in prayer. Perhaps her most effective prayers took place each morning at Burnley Shirt Factory. Sitting at her buttonhole machine, in the noisy den of machines revving up for the day's work, while bosses took last draws from their hand-rolled cigarettes and shouted orders, Mom sent up a silent plea: "Dear God, take care of my children today. Please keep them safe." As those invisible prayers cut through the smoky noise and headed straight up to Heaven, God's response was to build a wall of protection around two little kids while they walked to school on a busy highway. Those prayers also painted a protective covering over our doorpost when my brother and I came home after school and waited for Mom. Some of our neighbors were unemployed people who staggered alarmingly close to our front door, but we were never kidnapped nor molested, because our mother had us covered in prayer.

Mom led us up the tall steps of Southside Baptist Church every Sunday morning. We entered the double doors and walked into the quiet coolness of the sanctuary, where I looked around for God; Mom said He would be there. She often repeated to us the pastor's message when we arrived at home.

My mother believed that every dollar she earned making buttonholes belonged to God and that if she gave Him the first ten percent of her paycheck, He would stretch the rest to meet all of our needs. On one occasion, she accidentally dropped an envelope containing her tithe into the trash can. When she realized what had happened, she ran outside to search through the garbage. To her horror, she found the dented metal can empty and the garbage truck long-gone. Tears stung her eyes as she looked around, scanning the sidewalk and the grass and shrubs at the end of the walk. Then she spotted a white envelope wedged in the thick branches of a shrub. She pulled it out to find God's money safe inside.

As I glance back from an older woman's perspective now, I realize that Mom must have often felt inadequate for the task of motherhood.

Nevertheless, it was that inadequacy that sent her back to her knees over and over again to ask for help. And that is the priceless lesson she taught her children—that we are never really adequate for this life without the nurturing guidance of the heavenly Father.

On an Ordinary Day

> *JESUS prayed: "Holy Father, protect them by the power of your Name, the Name You give me—so that they may be one."*
> –John 17:11

On ordinary days, when we move through our world doing familiar things, we seldom question the location of God. Yet, on those days, we could be just moments from the unexpected—a breath away from an occurrence that could change our lives forever. That is when we need to know where God can be found.

It was one of those ordinary football Saturdays, a warm October day, as we tramped through the square in Oxford, Mississippi. The sidewalks were bulging with chattering, laughing people. College girls tottered in stiletto heels, and older men and women sported new sweaters, too warm for the humid day. We walked under a balcony, alive with laughter and the clink of ice-cubes, on our way to Square Books. The book store was, as usual, jammed with book-lovers, the aroma of coffee permeating the place where Willie Morris, John Grisham and many other famous writers have had book-signings. Out on the street again, we passed William Faulkner, sitting with pipe in hand, his steely eyed statue watching the happy parade of Auburn and Ole Miss fans traipsing by. My husband and our two sons, Mike and Rick, were taking part in a familiar scene, ending our walk through the quaint, old-fashioned town with a tailgate picnic. We ambled across campus toward the stadium and waited for friends to arrive before joining the jostling crowd to enter the stadium. For three hours we were up and down, clapping and cheering.

When the game was over, though our team had lost, we strolled happily to our van and prepared for the drive back home.

We had just repeated our ritual in the ordinary way, a tradition begun many years ago when our sons were young. My husband's only regret was that the grandchildren were not able to go with us this time; we had no indication that later we would be thankful they had not. There was no hint that our lives would be threatened that Halloween night. We bought gas at a curb store, said a simple prayer for traveling safety, and my husband drove onto the highway.

Mike sprawled across the back seat and quickly fell asleep. While listening to my husband and Rick rehash the game plays, I stretched my seat belt so that I could recline on the middle seat and eased into a drowsy, relaxed state. At 12:30 A.M., Rick's shouts woke me from a sound sleep. "Dad, Dad, wake up!" Our vehicle was lurching violently from one side of the road to the other, as though a huge hand had taken control and was intent on shaking us to pieces. My mind shouted, *"Lord, we prayed for safe travel. Did you hear?"* Certain that our lives were at stake, I closed my eyes and mumbled, "Jesus, Jesus, Jesus!" We left the roadand rolled over once, twice, maybe three times, steel grinding against steal, our bodies bouncing and slamming with each impact. Finally, our wild, angry ride came to a halt, and there was silence.

We were right side up, leaning into a ravine in the interstate median. We sat in a dazed state, surrounded by shattered glass. In front of me, my husband and Rick, still fastened in seat belts, appeared to be ok, but as I looked back toward the rear seat, the space where Mike had been sleeping moments before was empty.

Before I could voice my fear, Mike appeared outside the car beside my smashed window, and then he fell backward and lay motionless on the ground. Suddenly, voices spoke in the darkness, "We called an ambulance. Are you alright?" I answered, "My son is there on the ground. Help him!" I unfastened my seatbelt and tried to crawl out of the car and make my way to Mike. A voice said, "No!" as arms motioned me back into the vehicle. Two young men were beside Mike, instructing him, "Lie still. Don't move your head."

Some time later, I heard sirens and the sound of crushed glass as the ambulance attendants pushed a board underneath my body and moved me into the emergency vehicle. I was shaking, and someone put a warm blanket over me. Pressure against my chest caused my breathing to be labored; someone's hands placed an oxygen mask over my face. A voice explained that they would have to cut my clothes in order to examine my wounds. While scissors ripped through my new red vest, I asked, "Where is my son?" a female voice answered, "Don't worry. He's in another ambulance." More questions flooded my fuzzy mind, and again I tried to speak, but my voice was drowned in the rumble of the ambulance, as we bumped along the highway. *Was Mike hurting? Was he conscious? How had he gotten out of the car? Oh, Dear God, was he thrown out? Could he have internal injuries?*

Three Sundays later, as my broken ribs and shoulder were healing, I answered the phone. Mike was calling from a taxi while riding with his family through Chicago. "Hey, Mother, tell Dad we just passed Soldier Field, and now we're going past Lake Michigan. Pete wants to talk to you." Tears of gratitude came silently when I heard my grandson's excited voice describing his Thanksgiving vacation. It was an extraordinary Sunday for giving thanks that Pete's dad was alive and well and able to take him on that trip.

Thank God that what our eyes see on an ordinary day is only part of what is actually there. Mike, who was not wearing a seat-belt on the night of the crash, was thrown out of the car through the back window of the van. He found shards of glass in his pockets but did not have a scratch on his body, nor did he have broken bones. Apparently, God surrounded us with angels, and they caught Mike when he was thrown from the van. The voices in the darkness were "angels on earth," medical students who just happened to be in the car behind us on the highway.

Our very lives were beyond our control that night. Nevertheless, in the midst of the darkest night, when our feelings insisted that God had abandoned us, He was in complete control. I am thankful for God's angels on earth, who do His bidding on ordinary days and on life-threatening nights.

Building a Bridge to Heaven

And the Lord, He is the One who goes before you. He will be with you. He will not leave you nor forsake you; do not fear nor be dismayed.
           —Deuteronomy 31:8

My first grandchild, three-year-old Katie, leaned forward in her car seat and craned her neck so as to catch my eye. "Grandmamma, what are you saying?" she asked.

I was wedged in the center lane of traffic, trying to see the car in front of me. Heavy sheets of rain washed across the windshield while the wipers worked double time. Eighteen-wheelers passed on both sides of me, throwing up tidal waves, making it hard to see the signs ahead. I was afraid I would be unable to see my highway connection and would miss it. So, I was secretly praying with my eyes wide open, not realizing that my lips were moving. Katie's innocent little voice relaxed my stern face, and I smiled. "I'm praying, Katie, praying that God will get us safely through this storm."

Fifteen years later, my Katie is on her way to college, and I'm still praying for God to take her safely through this life. The prayers that began when she was being formed in her mother's womb are endless, and most of my prayers for her, her sister, Molly, and her brother, Pete, are spoken silently for only God to hear.

Someday soon, I'll tell my first grandchild everything I've learned about prayer—the greatest link we have from this earth to heaven. It is the connection that Jesus modeled for us when He got up early and went out to a lonely place to pray and receive direction from His heavenly Father. Perhaps I will say:

"Katie, I think the habit of prayer gets passed down from one generation to another. I watched my mother, your Gran-Gran, on her knees many times, her mouth moving quietly. She prayed about everything; nothing was too big or too small to talk to God about. I believe that God was just as real to her in her bedroom or at the breakfast table as He was in church. As a divorced parent, Mother was wholly responsible for her children's welfare. The task was too big for one woman, but her parents had taught her to turn to God. I know that her petitions kept me, her sometimes rebellious teenage daughter, from disaster. Her prayers also brought her son out of a jungle in Vietnam, and later, her prayers took him from alcoholism to sobriety. I watched my mother pray, and I went with her to church. I saw God as someone in the distant sky, someone to be respected, for sure, but I prayed only when I was in trouble. Even then, I wondered if God was really listening. Nevertheless, Mother's quiet prayers were like a slow marinating process that eventually drew me into a closer relationship with her God.

After I married your grandad, and we experienced the blessing of your dad's birth, we eagerly searched for heavenly help. What a responsibility we had! There were no parenting classes back then, and we made so many mistakes. I suspect that prayer was the only useful thing we knew how to do when we were young parents. "Because of your Gran-Gran's prayers for me, I came to believe there was an unseen world around us, inhabited by angels sent by God to both protect me and nudge me. Sometimes, the angels closed doors I wasn't meant to enter; sometimes, they opened doors and escorted me safely along the pathway that God planned for me. I have always believed that their help in my life was the direct result of prayer. It is prayer that builds a bridge to heaven, a bridge that ends with God holding the gate wide open.

Katie, when you were three years old, your family could control so much of your life. But now we can't fasten you into the seatbelt and take you where we want you to go. You are the driver now. You have a good foundation of faith, having been trained in the way you should go. So, we pray that you will build your own bridges to Heaven now. We ask

God to take you safely through all the storms, to send angels to guide you, and to open the highways that you should travel. And most of all, we pray you will know that your heavenly Father is always with you, even on the darkest night."

Asking

You do not have because you do not ask.
—James 4:2

On a Sunday night, at Highland Methodist Church, I walked down the aisle and knelt at the altar to pray. It must have been after one of those stirring sermons from the Book of James on "Faith without works is dead," when I felt a strong urge to do something more with my life to prove that I was a Christian. So, I whispered, "Lord, give me a ministry; I want to do something for you."

God had already prepared a petite, silver-haired lady to visit Highland Church. Within weeks of my prayer, Miss Wright found her way to 20th Street and 35th Avenue in Meridian, Mississippi, armed with Bible and flannel board to present the Child Evangelism Program. After she approached our pastor, Reverend Wolfe issued an invitation for church members to attend a demonstration of Good News Club. The pastor's wife and I were the only ones who responded.

As I sat in the training class watching Miss Wright tell the Bible stories, I knew this was the answer to my prayer. But like Moses, I argued, *I'm slow of speech, Lord... I don't think I can do it... This is not what I had in mind!*

Nevertheless, I knew God was opening a door for me. I felt totally inadequate. I was afraid I would fail and look stupid, but I was more afraid of not obeying God. So, I got my own flannel board and a book of flannelgraph figures that had to be cut out like paper dolls and headed for Wesley House Community Center to do an after-school class for children.

Right away, those children began responding to the Word of God, and week by week, many of them received Christ as their Savior. My own two boys were greatly affected and made their own professions of faith due to their exposure to Good News Club. All along, I was learning more and more about the Bible, and my own faith was growing.

Wesley House occupied an old, two-story house in a poor, aging neighborhood. The children gathered around me in the front room for sessions of Good News Club. People entering the building would sometimes pause and listen to the Bibles stories. I was amazed at the expressions on adult faces; they were absorbing the message of God's Word as if they had never heard it presented in such a simple way.

Today, I often run into my former students, who are now middle-aged. I love it when one of them reminds me of an image gleaned from those Bible stories so many years ago. I am so glad I prayed that simple prayer that brought Miss Wright to tell us about the Gospel that even a little child can understand. I am especially thankful that today my son and his wife are now carrying on the Child Evangelism tradition by conducting Good News Clubs in downtown Jackson, Mississippi.

SCARY PLACES

HE sent His Word and healed them, and delivered them from their destructions.
—Psalm 107:20

My husband squeezed my hand as we exited the car, walked through the musty parking garage, and entered the elevator to the medical clinic. My fate depended on the words written inside a manila folder upstairs on the fourth floor.

We sat in a small examining room, listening intently for footsteps outside the door. A giant eye glared at us from a poster on the wall as we made small talk and exchanged anxious winks and smiles. After my watch's second hand made twenty-eight unhurried rotations, footsteps paused outside, and I heard the rattle of the basket on the other side of the door as my chart was lifted. Finally, the doctor walked in with stern eyes and a stiff smile. Before he spoke, I knew, but I wasn't prepared to hear the words that stripped me of all hope: "Mrs. Dawkins, I'm sorry. The lab report indicates that I removed a malignant melanoma from your eye."

Tom groaned, "No!" The color drained from his face, and his knuckles turned gray. I searched my limp brain for a magic word to erase the anguish in my husband's voice and to dispel the tension in that tiny, windowless room. Yet, nothing could wipe out the effect of those two overpowering words: malignant melanoma. So began the adventure in which God would expose my insecurities and test my faith. He would call attention to my desperate need for His Word and my need for other people.

I knew God was not sleeping when the angry red lesion attached itself firmly at the edge of my iris. I belong to Him, and He keeps me in full view at all times. I was sure He had a plan for what was happening, yet fear held me in its icy grip, because I could not see what He had in mind or what He would require of me. I only knew one thing: I was inadequate.

My doctor was a graduate of Johns Hopkins Medical School. He was an excellent surgeon, but what I liked best about him was that he knew God. He grimaced at the sight of the monster in my eye as we discussed the possibilities at my first appointment. Yes, he could remove it, but there was the risk of impairing my sight, and worst of all: there were blood vessels leading into it, indicating a threat to more than my eye. After much consideration, we reached a decision. "Ok," I said, "let's schedule the surgery, and we'll pray that God will bless the work of your hands." The doctor responded, "Please do. I always pray before doing surgery; there's Someone wiser than me up there."

So, here we were, a week past surgery, and though my eye was intact and my vision normal, we sat reeling with the reality of cancer. The doctor moved closer, placed a sympathetic hand on my shoulder, and said, "I'm not sure what we're dealing with. There's still something there that needs to be removed. With your permission, I will send the x-rays to Johns Hopkins and get their advice before doing anything else."

Tom and I held each other up as we left the examining room, entered the elevator, and descended to the gloomy parking garage. We got in our car and drove out into the street as a light rain misted the windshield. The sunlight of that chilly February day had disappeared, and with it, went our hope. The days ahead would drag on, and the battle in my mind would rage.

Fear, my midnight visitor, caused me to cower under the covers. I never feared dying, but I was afraid to suffer under conditions that seemed inevitable. This fear grew larger and strangled my faith. I was sure I could not measure up to the bravery I had witnessed in others who had dealt with cancer. My beautiful, young friend, Lynn, was the most recent example. She wore her pain courageously, and her faith endured to the end. I wondered how Lynn had managed that. And, dare I even think it—why had God allowed it? I felt that God vanished the day Lynn died. These secret memories flooded my mind.

I leaned on Tom's arm as we walked into the oncology building, a place where people are transported on wheels—patients in wheelchairs, and weak pale bodies on rolling beds. I heard a child's cry and looked toward the door, where a nurse was taking a little boy from his mother's arms. I saw a young woman curled in a fetal position on a hospital gurney. She was oblivious to her surrounds, helpless and frail. I felt a strange connection to her; though my body was not confined to a hospital gurney, my spirit lay helpless, my faith paralyzed.

I was much like the paralytic in the Bible story who needed someone else's faith—someone to take hold of the stretcher, carry him up on the roof, tear a hole in it, and lower him at Jesus' feet. Similarly, I was dependent upon the strength of others.

As I lay in this helpless state night after night, something began to happen that I could not see or feel. When I could not pray for myself, intercessions rose to the heavens. As those pleas entered the gates of heaven and accumulated at the throne of God, my bed, like the paralytic's mat, was moved on a secret journey, taking me closer to the feet of Jesus. As my friends and family prayed, God sent out his nudging angels to prompt people to do amazing things. One Sunday in church, Nita, my quiet friend, sat down on the pew beside me and handed me a cassette tape containing Scriptures. I began listening to those faith-building words at night when I could not sleep:

"Jesus touched their eyes; and instantly they received their sight..."
"Great throngs accompanied Him; He healed them all..."
"I Am the Lord who heals you..."
"Behold, I will not forget you. I have indelibly imprinted you on the palm of each of my hands..."

Did God really have me imprinted in the palm of His Hands? Would He hold me there, securely, no matter what happened? Gradually, the Scriptures transformed my mind, driving out the darkness of doubt and filling me with an awareness of God's presence. I began to feel His love, and I knew I could trust my future to Him.

When we finally heard from my doctor, he told us that the experts at Johns Hopkins had advised him to perform a second surgery, and then a third. After the final procedure, the lab report returned, stating that no malignancy was present, and my oncologist reported similar findings! In my secret thoughts I was journeying alone. Nevertheless, God was always there. I remembered the doctor's words: "There is Someone wiser than me up there." That Someone was the only one who knew my secret thoughts, the only one who could see the darkness surrounding my mind. When I was weak, He sent people to carry my mat and lift me out of the shadows, into the sunlight, where I could see clearly that I was at the feet of the Healer.

Ageless Spirit

Do you not know that you are a temple of God, and the Spirit of God dwells in you?
—1 Corinthians 6:19

We followed her as she wheeled her rolling walker down the wide carpeted hallway, a petite woman immaculately dressed in a stylish pantsuit with a matching ribbon, tied gracefully around her snowy-white hair. She led us to a door that seemed more like that of an upscale hotel and welcomed us into a charming room full of antiques. We sat like ladies at a tea party hosted by Mamma Starnes, in her cozy room at the assisted living home. When the nurse peeped in to ask if we needed anything, I am sure she saw only a little old lady with two younger women, but there was another presence in that room, unseen, yet felt and heard.

My friend Barbara and I had driven to Madison, Mississippi, in search of a very unique lady who had a special connection to the Lord. Barbara had said, "You've got to meet her. Mamma Starnes is one hundred and two, but she still prays for our family. When she prays for people, they are healed. They say she has Alzheimer's, but you'll not believe it. She's sharp as a tack."

So, we took our problems and our prayer list and received an instant dose of faith—the best therapy I had had in years. Mamma Starnes quoted scriptures and prayed as though the Lord Himself was sitting in a chair beside her. She laid a gentle hand on my shoulder and said, "Give it all to the Lord, honey. He knows what to do. It's going to be alright." And then, just briefly, her mind seemed to slip into another time zone of the past where she began talking about her immediate need to rush home and prepare the evening meal for her husband, although he had been dead for over thirty years. Nevertheless, that tiny senior moment failed to diminish the integrity of her spirit. Her one hundred and two-year-old brain might have been worn with age, yet her spirit reflected that of the ageless Holy Spirit.

Mamma Starnes died when she was one hundred and five or, rather, she slipped over into the heavenly realm. Every prayer she prayed for me was answered, and everything she told me eventually came true. That beautiful lady opened my eyes to the reality of the spirit world. We bypassed her natural wisdom and conversed in that invisible world of the Holy Spirit. Her words came not from her physical brain but from the Holy Spirit—the Jesus Spirit.

Uncle Nelson

And they had golden bowls full of incense, which are the prayers of God's People.
—Revelation 5:8

Around three o'clock on Sunday afternoon, I would key in the numbers and sit back and wait for the cold, impersonal answer machine message: "You have reached the Nelson residence. Who are you, and what do you want?" After the beep, I'd identify myself, and as though his hand had been waiting to lift the receiver, there would be an immediate response: "Hello, Mary Virginia, how are you?"

My ninety-eight-year-old Uncle set strong boundaries around his life. He trusted no one, and he would not open his door to visitors. He was suspicious of doctors and neighbors, and he certainly did not trust God. If anything, he was angry at a God whom he deemed responsible for the years of loneliness he had endured since his wife died of Alzheimer's.

His only connection to the outside world was the occasional trip with his maid to the grocery store, phone calls from two or three relatives, and his wide-screen television set. He was convinced that the computer world was a Communistic conspiracy; he warned me that anything tagged with "dot com" was extremely dangerous.

Having prayed for Uncle Nelson for sixteen years, my faith was fading. He would be ninety-nine on his next birthday. He had health problems which he stubbornly refused to deal with. I wondered how he could live much longer, and I knew he wasn't ready to die. I had written him a letter complete with scripture and a detailed plan for salvation, later to find that he was highly insulted. And when he lay helpless in bed after breaking his hip, I had stood by his bed and asked to pray for him; he dismissed my offer with an icy "No, go home and pray if you want to, but it won't do any good."

One day, I mentioned this while speaking to a women's group. I told the group about our ongoing family prayers for my uncle. My friend, Christy, approached me afterward and said that she might be able to help. Her brother-in-law pastored a church near my uncle's neighborhood. Maybe he could visit my uncle.

I approached my uncle with renewed hope and asked, "Would you let a friend of mine come for a visit?" The answer was, "Maybe, but have him call first." Pastor Henson called and called, but Uncle Nelson refused to take the calls.

Now, my compassion turned to anger at this stubborn man. Why did I care? Why couldn't I just give up and let it go? There was obviously nothing more I could do. Nevertheless, every morning when I faced his name on my prayer list, I knew if I didn't pray for him no one else would.

One Sunday, when I made the usual phone call, there was no answer. Uncle Nelson was in the hospital, and it was determined that even if his condition improved, he could no longer live at home alone. Against his furious protests, Uncle Nelson was moved to an assisted living home. On my first visit to Peachtree Village Retirement Home, I was struck with the thought that in this new environment, my stubborn uncle was no longer able to maintain his privacy. All barriers, except for the ones in his mind, had fallen away. Nurses, aides, and volunteers made their way in and out of his room several times a day. I was hopeful once more; this would be a perfect place for the pastor to visit.

Pastor Henson was eager for the challenge, and he had a new plan. He would send Mr. Ray Downey, a retired professor of English, who was an expert at leading people to the Lord. It seemed to be a perfect plan; the two retired professors would have so much in common.

Mr. Ray Downey, with his disarming smile and gentle voice, made an easy entrance into my Uncle's life, paying several visits to the retirement home. Uncle Nelson was friendly toward him, but each time the conversation got around to the topic of faith in God, my uncle abruptly changed the subject and began one of his long story-telling sessions. A reoccurring story was about a dog. For some reason, Uncle Nelson was obsessed with the memory of a dog that had once inhabited his neighborhood.

On the third visit, Mr. Downey was discouraged when Uncle Nelson began again his saga of the neighborhood dog. Suddenly, in the midst of the story, the door burst open and two dogs ran into the room. They came to a halt in front of Uncle Nelson's chair and stood peacefully gazing into the old man's eyes. No one knew where they had come from, or why they would come to this particular room at that exact moment. I believe a glimmer of light flashed inside a lonely old man's head when the dogs came to rest at his feet. Perhaps my uncle knew that this unusual happening was God's exclamation point to a story that mattered. Ray Downey and Uncle Nelson began to laugh, and with the laughter the final barrier between the two professors melted away. That night, I received a surprising e-mail that brought tears to my eyes: "Dear Virginia, tonight your uncle, Dr. C.O. Nelson, prayed to receive Jesus as Savior."

Shortly after, when my husband and I visited my uncle, he welcomed our prayers. Three months later, when we celebrated his ninety-ninth birthday, it was very noticeable that his mind was failing. Three more months, and Uncle Nelson passed into eternity.

Only God knew why the dog story was so important to my uncle. I did not know, and certainly Mr. Ray Downey didn't know until the dogs ran into room B-7 at Peachtree Village Retirement Home.

I will forever be grateful that in response to prayers, God arranged circumstances, nudged people, and even sent two dogs on a mission to accomplish His purposes.

Prayers For Betty Jo

Then Jesus touched their eyes, saying, 'According to your faith let it be to you.' And their eyes were opened.
–Matthew 9:29-30

My beautiful cousin, Betty Jo, was nurtured in the Jewish faith, educated at the University of Oklahoma, married, and raised two fine sons. Betty was a God-seeker. In her late fifties, when diagnosed with Alzheimer's, she continued her quest for God. She told me she wanted to do one last thing before she died—she wanted to go to Israel. Knowing this, her son, Max, took her to the prayer wall in Jerusalem, where she placed her written prayers in a crevice of the wall.

Family was very important to Betty, so after her mom, my Aunt Lucille, passed away, she flew from her home in Dallas several times to visit with us in Mississippi. Aunt Lucille was buried in Meridian, and Betty always took flowers to the gravesite when she came.

On one occasion, shortly after the burial, a special ceremony was to be held at the gravesite in memory of Aunt Lucille. Betty, being the next of kin, would be responsible for leading the responsive reading at the memorial gathering. A few days before the service, she sat on my couch and began her practice reading; I noticed that she became very frustrated. When I tried to help her with the words, I saw what was happening; she was able to read the very first line effectively, but when she came to the second line, her eyes refused to return to the left side of the page, they went to the middle of the page instead. She tried over and over again, but the words were not making sense—Betty became tearful.

Our church was due to host a "Healing Service" where the ministers would pray for the sick. When I asked Betty if she would like to go with me and get prayer, she immediately said yes. The next day, I walked down the aisle with Betty where a retired medical doctor, Dr. James Graham, was ministering prayer. We explained Betty's situation as well as her reading problem, and Dr. Graham said, "The reading problem sounds like something similar to dyslexia. Something is going on in the brain that prevents you from reading properly, Betty." He then prayed, asking God to heal her.

When we arrived home, Betty picked up a paperback book, and as she read, the words began making sense. She shouted, "I can read! I can read!" She was then able to practice the memorial reading properly. Later, she called her friend, and I overheard her say, "Lauren, I went to Mary Virginia's church, and a man healed me." I interrupted and said, "No, Betty. That man did not heal you. He prayed, asking God to heal you, in the name of Jesus. When Jesus walked as a man on earth, He healed many people—it was Jesus who took the confusion away and enabled you to read." Betty responded, "Well, Jesus was Jewish, you know!"

The next day, Betty was able to successfully lead the responsive reading at the gravesite. Later, she came once again to our church service where Pastor Giles prayed for her complete healing. Alzheimer's eventually took Betty's life, but I believe it was those prayers, and the of her family that enabled Betty to recognize her sons and interact with her loved-ones to the very end of her life.

Chapter Two

How To Pray

Now it came to pass, as He was praying in a certain place, when He ceased, that one of His disciples said to Him, "Lord teach us to pray, as John also taught his disciples.
–Luke 11:1

THE MODEL PRAYER

So, He said to them, *"When you pray, say 'OUR FATHER,'* When you come to God in prayer, you do not come to a stranger who *needs* an introduction, or to an enemy who is against you. You do not come to a statue that you cannot see or hear, or to some mean and impersonal deity. You come to your Father, whose heart reaches out to you in goodness and kindness. He wants you to come as a child who is loved, accepted, cared for, and who is secure. He waits to hear your prayer.

"WHICH ART IN HEAVEN" God is a person who lives in a bright, beautiful, glorious place. through prayer, you can gather the riches of heaven and bring them down to earth.

"HALLOWED BE THY NAME" He is the great and mighty One, King of kings, Lord of lords, Prince of Peace. Honor His name.

"THY KINGDOM COME" The Kingdom of God consists of God's words and ways, His character and nature, His majesty and glory, and His authority and power. His words will change how you think, and His character will change how you live.

"THY WILL BE DONE ON EARTH, AS IT IS IN HEAVEN" Prayer is not pleading with God to do something that He is against. Confident prayer comes by wanting the things that God wants for your life. We may read the Bible and learn what God wants for us.

"GIVE US THIS DAY OUR DAILY BREAD" God is the giver of all things, not just bread, but grace, wisdom, and peace. He meets physical and spiritual needs.

"AND FORGIVE US OUR DEBTS AS WE FORGIVE OUR DEBTORS" Jesus has forgiven me. I must forgive others who have hurt me.

"AND LEAD US NOT INTO TEMPTATION" I may be tempted to sin, but temptation is not sin. I can say "No" to the temptation. God will give me a way of escape.

"BUT DELIVER US FROM EVIL" Prayer is your song of freedom and declaration of deliverance from the powers of the Evil one.

"FOR THINE IS THE KINGDOM, AND THE POWER, AND THE GLORY" No one is higher than God. He is above all things. Nothing is impossible for Him.

Rules For Prayer

Wherever the soul of man turns, unless toward God, it cleaves to sorrow, even though the things outside God and outside itself to which it cleaves may be things of beauty.
—Augustine, *Confessions*

Timothy Keller, in his book, *Prayer: Experiencing Awe and Intimacy with God,* shares John Calvin's "Rules for Prayer." Calvin's first rule is reverence or the Fear of God. This does not mean that we should be afraid of God. Rather, reverential fear means that we are aware of the privilege of coming before the Almighty God of the universe. We are moved by God's majesty and seek to honor and obey Him. However, Keller explains, *"A Christian should be intensely concerned not to grieve or dishonor the one who is so glorious and who did so much for us."* Keller adds *"The very fact that we have access to God's attention and presence should concentrate the thoughts and elevate the heart."*

Calvin's second rule for prayer is "The sense of need or spiritual humility." We must realize our dependence on God as well as a readiness to recognize and repent of our own faults. Calvin simply tells us to "drop all pretense, to flee from all phoniness." Confession and repentance are necessary.

Calvin's third and fourth rules for prayer are considered together: submissive trust and confident hope. We are reminded that "we have not because we ask not," but that God will not give us anything contrary to His will. Matthew 7:7 tells us, "Ask and you shall receive." God tempers the outcome with His wisdom. We must rest in His will.

Calvin's fifth rule is the rule of grace. In Jesus' name, we come to God, not on our merits but on the basis of undeserved mercy. To pray in Jesus' name means to come to God in prayer consciously, trusting in Christ for our salvation and not relying on our own credibility or record. God our Father is committed to the good of His children.

The Prince of Preachers

My conviction is that prayer is the grandest power in the entire universe. It has more omnipotent force than any other force known to mankind.
–Charles Spurgeon

Charles Spurgeon was called the "Prince of Preachers" by his peers. He led the congregation of London's Metropolitan Tabernacle as it grew into the world's largest independent congregation during the Nineteenth Century. He believed it was the power of prayer that built that ministry. When people visited Metropolitan Tabernacle, he would take them to the basement prayer room, where people were always on their knees interceding for the church, and he would say, "here is the powerhouse of the church."

Of his sixty-three volumes of sermons, many were on the subject of prayer. Spurgeon said, "My own soul's conviction is that prayer is the grandest power in the entire universe. It has more omnipotent force than any other force known to mankind. Prayer has as true, as real, as invaluable an influence over the entire universe as any of the laws of matter."

Spurgeon often quoted Hebrews 4:16: "Let us come boldly unto the throne, that we may obtain mercy, and find grace to help in time of need." He explained that when we come to the throne of grace, our prayers are no longer received into a place of absolute justice, but to a place where God meets sinners through the blood of Jesus Christ, and there, our desires are interpreted by the Holy Spirit.

On the matter of diligence, he says, "Stones are broken by an earnest use of the hammer, and the stone mason usually goes down on his knees. Use the hammer of diligence and let the knee of prayer be exercised. You may force your way through anything with the leverage of prayers." Spurgeon often used the Biblical example in Daniel 10 as a reason for continued diligence: Daniel spent three weeks fasting and praying. And then God sent an angel to say: "Fear not, Daniel, for from the first day that you set your mind and heart to understand and to humble yourself before your God, your words were heard, and I have come as a consequence of your words."

Spurgeon preached that we can most often know the will of God when we familiarize ourselves with the Word of God, which has many precious promises that we can claim. He says, "When you plead His promises, then your will is his will." He emphasizes that God is delighted with the prayers of His children; He collects those prayers in golden bowls, and our prayers are as sweet as incense to God.

This was Spurgeon's final admonition to the saints regarding prayer: "We have only to pray. All things are possible to us. Pray. You have the key in the door of heaven—keep it there and turn it till the gate shall open. Pray, for prayer holds the chain that binds the dragon. Prayer can hold fast and restrain even Satan himself. Pray. God girds you with omnipotence if you know how to pray. May we not fail here, but may the Spirit of God strengthen us, and to God shall be the glory forever and ever."

Try Prayer Power

Set aside a few minutes every day. Do not say anything. Simply practice thinking about God. This will make your mind spiritually receptive.
—Dr. Norman Vincent Peale

In 1952, Dr. Norman Vincent Peale wrote *The Power of Positive Thinking*. In the preface of his book he states, "The dynamic laws which this book teaches were learned the hard way, by trial and error, in my personal search for a way of life. The book is my effort to share my spiritual experience; for if it helped me, I felt it might also be of help to others. I found my own answers in the teachings of Jesus Christ." With the first printing, *The Power of Positive Thinking* sold millions of copies. Within this classic book, is a chapter devoted to the power of prayer. Peale believed that prayer was the greatest power available to the individual, and that every problem could be solved through prayer. He believed this to be true even in the process of old age, saying, "Prayer power seems able even to normalize the aging process, by limiting infirmity and deterioration. It is not necessary to allow your spirit to sag or grow stale or dull. Furthermore, prayer could lessen the weakness and listlessness resulting from accumulating years."

Describing our brains as having about two billion little storage batteries, Dr. Peale says, "The human brain can send off power by thoughts and prayers." He speaks of what he calls "flash" prayers or "shooting" prayers—the process of sending out vibrations from one person to another and then to God. He experimented with this while traveling across the country by train and praying for people he saw along the way. He prayed for a man plowing a field and a woman hanging clothes to dry. In one train station, he saw a man leaning against a wall. "I prayed that he would wake up," said Peale, "and get off welfare and amount to something." He saw a lovable little kid, one pant leg longer than the other, wearing an oversized sweater, hair tousled, and having dirt on his face. Peale prayed for him, and as the train started to move away from the station, the little boy looked up and gave Peale a wonderful smile and then waved to him. "I shall never see that boy again," says Peale, "but our lives touched, and I am sure it was because the power of God was moving in a circuit through me, to the boy and back to God."

Dr. Peale's Ten Rules for Effective Prayer

1. Set aside a few minutes each day. Do not say anything. Simply practice thinking about God. This will make your mind spiritually receptive.
2. Then, pray orally, using simple, natural words. Tell God anything that is on your mind. Do not think you must use stereotyped pious phrases. Talk to God in your own language. He understands it.

3. Pray as you go about the business of the day, on the subway or bus or at your desk. Utilize minute prayers by closing your eyes to shut out the world and concentrating briefly on God's presence.
4. Do not always ask when you pray, but instead affirm that God's blessings are being given, and spend most of your prayers giving thanks.
5. Pray with the belief that sincere prayers can reach out and surround your loved ones with God's love and protection.
6. Never use a negative thought in prayer. Positive thoughts get results.
7. Always express willingness to accept God's will. Ask for what you want but be willing to take what God gives you. It may be better than what you ask for.
8. Practice the attitude of putting everything in God's hands. Ask for the ability to do your best and to leave the results to God.
9. Pray for people you do not like or who have mistreated you. Resentment is blockade number one of spiritual power.
10. Make a list and pray for others.

INTERCESSORY PRAYER

The effective, fervent prayer of a righteous man avails much. Elijah was a man with a nature like ours, and he prayed earnestly that it would not rain; and it did not rain on the land for three years and six months. And he prayed again, and the heaven gave rain, and the earth produced its fruit.
—James 5:16-18

Intercessory Prayer, written by Pastor Dutch Sheets, tells the story of a comatose woman with a tracheotomy in her throat and a feeding tube in her stomach. She had been confined to a nursing home bed for a year and a half. Doctors gave the woman no hope for living, no chance of coming out of the coma; they said even if she did, she would live in a vegetative state.

Sheets was shocked when he first realized how critical the situation actually was, but he had made a promise to a relative of the comatose woman that he would pray. He traveled several miles to the nursing facility every week for a period of one year. Toward the end of the year, he saw no change in the patient's condition but he sensed that God was saying, "I sent you. Don't quit."

The woman's condition eventually worsened. She was sent to a hospital for treatment for an infection, where the doctors advised the family that she would soon die. Miraculously, three days later, She woke up with full restoration to her brain; she was praising God.

Sheets reminds us that even though God is sovereign, He wants us to pray; our prayers are used to bring about God's will to earth. Theologian Andrew Murray said: "God is inseparably connected with our asking. Only by intercession can that power be brought down from heaven which will enable the church to conquer the world."

Sheets reminds us of the persistence of men like Elijah and Daniel. When Elijah prayed for rain, as chronicled in the first book of Kings, his prayers brought rain when there had been none for three and a half years. In the book of Daniel, chapter ten, we see that Daniel prayed for twenty-one days without seeing any results; and then, God sent an angel to say that his prayers had been heard on the very first day.

Sheets suggests that sometimes it takes an accumulation of prayers; in the Book of Revelation, we are told that our prayers are collected in "Golden Bowls." Sheets believes that even though God is all powerful and sufficient, He still uses our prayers to accomplish His will on earth.

Sheets gives us hope for wayward children with this story:

David and Polly, members of Pastor Sheets church, prayed for their son before he was born and they raised him in the church. But when Jonathan was seventeen, he began to wander away from God. He soon began a life of total rebellion, doing drugs and adopting an addictive lifestyle. Being a diabetic, he would often end up in the hospital, only to get out and go back to drugs.

David and Polly asked their friends to pray with them for their wayward son. Together, they would ask the Holy Spirit to hover over Jonathan's bed as he slept, and in his car when he drove. They did this daily. They would anoint his room, his doors and windows, his bed, his car, and his clothing. Polly would often go into Jonathan's room and sing in the Spirit for an hour or more at a time; she sometimes prayed for four to six hours in the night, and she always spoke positive words over her son: "Jonathan has a destiny I know he will fulfill." In spite of all, things seemed to get worse; it was like Jonathan was on a mission to destroy his own life.

Nevertheless, they continued to pray, praying scriptures over the uncontrollable child. Polly said, "Throughout four years of intercession, the Lord taught us much about prayer and gave us great encouragement along the way. He even allowed my husband to see the angel that would ride in Jonathan's car everywhere he went; the angel was also with Jonathan when he spent a night in jail." Eventually, their prayers for Jonathan were answered. Polly said, "Jonathan prayed a prayer of re-commitment to Christ, and we watched in amazement as the things of the world began to fall away from Jonathan and then the things of the kingdom of God became clear and appealing. Does God answer prayer? You bet He does!"

Sheets reminds us that there is a veil that keeps unbelievers from clearly seeing the gospel: He cites 2 Corinthians 4:3-4, "And even if our gospel is veiled, it is veiled to those who are perishing, in whose case the god of this world (Satan) has blinded the minds of the unbelieving, that they might not see the light of the gospel of the glory of Christ, who is the image of God." Therefore, we have a part to play in lifting the veil off the mind of the unbeliever; our continued intercession is necessary.

Break Through Prayer

Prayer is not overcoming God's reluctance. It is laying hold of God's willingness.
—George Muller

Reverend Jim Cymbala is the pastor of the Brooklyn Tabernacle Church in New York City. In his book, *Break Through Prayer,* he gives guidelines for approaching God. "Prayer is not some kind of heavenly lottery," he says. "The Bible does not counsel us to pray with an 'I hope this will work' kind of attitude. Instead, we are told that prayer brings us before the throne of grace as children seeking the help of their heavenly Father."

- Approach God in and through Jesus' name. *We* make our appeal on the basis of what Jesus did for us rather than on our own merits. Only this path will lead to the prayer-hearing God.
- A person who prays must believe. In James 1:6 we are instructed: *"But let him ask in faith, with no doubting, for he who doubts is like a wave of the sea driven and tossed by the wind."*
- A clear conscience and a pure heart are absolute necessities for prevailing prayer. We cannot confidently ask God for answers when we cling to the sins that nailed Jesus to the cross of Calvary. *"If I regard wickedness in my heart, the Lord will not hear."*—Psalm 66:18

Patience

God's plan and His way of working out His plan are frequently beyond our ability to fathom and understand. We must learn to trust when we don't understand.
—Jerry Bridges

In his book *Hope for Each Day,* Billy Graham wrote about a woman who had prayed for her husband's conversion for ten years. She told Graham that she was losing hope, because it seemed that after all that prayer, he was further away from God than ever. Graham advises her to continue praying. Sometime later, he heard from the woman again; she told him that her husband had miraculously been saved in the eleventh year of her intercession.

Graham advises her: "Never stop praying, no matter how dark and hopeless your case may seem. Your responsibility isn't to tell God when He must act or even how He must act. Your responsibility is simply to pray without ceasing."

Graham's wife, Ruth, wrote the book *Prodigals and Those Who Love Them.* "It was early in the morning in another country," she writes. "I awoke around three o'clock. The name of someone I loved dearly flashed into my mind. It was like an electric shock. Instantly I was wide awake. I lay there and prayed for the one who was trying hard to run from God. When it is dark and the imagination runs wild, there are fears only a mother can understand. Suddenly, the Lord said to me, 'Quit studying the problem and start studying the promises.'" Ruth turned on the light, got out her Bible, and read Philippians 4:6: "Be careful for nothing; but in everything by prayer and supplication with thanksgiving let your requests be made known unto God." When the word "thanksgiving" stood out, she began giving thanks and praise to God.

In considering the stubborn will of those who are the object of loving, concerned prayer, Ruth Graham was encouraged when she read Proverbs 21:1: "The king's heart is in the hand of the Lord, as the rivers of water; He turns it wherever He wishes." Matthew Henry writes: "God can change men's minds, can turn them from that which they seemed most intent upon, as the husbandman, by canals and gutters, turns the water through his grounds, which does not alter the nature of the water, nor put any force upon it, any more than God's providence does upon the native freedom of man's will, but directs the course of it to serve His own purpose." Henry reminds us that our unceasing prayers are used by God to change the hearts of those we love.

George Muller's Prayers

During my lifetime I have had twenty-five thousand prayers answered—and five thousand of these answers came on the very day I made the petitions.
—George Muller

George Muller, founder of orphanages in England, left a prayer journal containing hundreds of requests logged in Nineteenth Century England. At the time of Muller's death, all recorded prayers had answers written beside them with the exception of two. The two unanswered prayers were requests for salvation for unsaved people. The story is told that one of these men received Jesus as his Savior at Muller's funeral. Apparently, Muller's prayers were still active, even after his death.

I envied Muller and wondered what was so different about him. What gave him such favor with God? Why did God answer his prayers while so many of my prayers seemed to get lost along the way? I read everything I could find on Muller's life, and this is what I learned:

After his spiritual conversion, Muller developed a special relationship with God, spending much time on his knees. He read the Bible every day, seeking the mind of God, and he sought to walk in obedience to God's commands. With this kind of interaction, God was able to drop His ideas and His best plans into Muller's heart. God gave this humble man a big dream—to build orphanages for the street children of Bristol, England, a need so great in a day when poor children were often treated little better than animals.

When Muller read the words of Psalm 81:10, *"Open your mouth wide and I will fill it,"* he knew that God had spoken directly to him, saying, "Just ask for what you need; there is no limit to My supply." Hence, Muller made a written prayer list. He asked for a house and furniture, people to care for the children, clothes for the children, food and money. Each day, Muller and his wife would pray secretly, telling no one of their needs. As they prayed over the list, the Holy Spirit impressed individuals to give money, donate houses, and volunteer their services. In this way, the once impossible dream began to materialize. Beginning with one donated building, eventually, there were seven buildings housing 2,000 children. In his lifetime, Muller raised millions of dollars. Never once did he advertise, solicit, or ask men for funds.

The orphanage project was a continual walk in faith. A typical day might begin without food for breakfast. Muller and the children would sit down to tables with empty plates and ask God to supply food. Shortly afterward, a knock at the door would reveal the Holy Spirit's nudging as someone had felt impressed to bring food that very hour.

During the first World War, when everything seemed darkest, God always arrived in time with a bountiful supply for the needs of the orphanage. While the banks closed, God sent in sufficient funds to purchase what might be necessary to feed the children. Muller was known for his successful prayer life. He meditated on scripture as a means of preparing his heart and leading it into prayer. He had a set of questions that he asked himself at each daily reading:

- Is there any example for me to follow?
- Is there any command for me to obey?
- Is there any error for me to avoid?
- Is there any sin for me to forsake?
- Is there any promise for me to claim?
- Is there any new thought about God Himself?

George Muller's Financial Advice

After each year's audit of Muller's orphanage project, a detailed report was made public showing how the Lord had provided. Businessmen were particularly interested in Muller's success. One such executive, whose firm was threatened with bankruptcy, traveled a considerable distance for an interview. This is the advice Muller gave him:

1. Each day you and your wife are to spread your business difficulties before the Lord and pray.
2. You are then to watch for answers to prayer and expect them.
3. Absolute honesty is necessary; avoid all business trickeries.
4. Beginning immediately, a certain proportion of your income must be given to God.
5. Keep a record, month by month, of how the Lord is dealing with you and what's happening.

The man followed this advice and kept a record which he sent to Muller monthly. During the first year, the man's business came out of the red and up some three thousand pounds over the previous year. According to Muller's journals, the businessman's profits continued to mount each year thereafter.

THE NAME OF JESUS

Jesus prayed, 'Holy Father, protect them by the power of your Name—the Name You gave me—so that they may be one.'
–John 17:11

You may ask anything in My Name, and I will do it.
—John 14:14

In 1980, I read Betty Malz's description of her visit to Heaven in *My Glimpse of Eternity*. I was amazed that a person could die, have his or her spirit lift from the body, ascend to heaven, and then return to a healed body. Betty Malz's description of Heaven matched the Biblical descriptions of the gates of pearl, the Light of Jesus, the throne room, and the streets of gold. This story made heaven more real to me, and my faith was strengthened. But it was the way she described prayer that painted a picture in my mind which I still see today; there were shafts of light lifting from houses and churches, which were the prayers of God's people, divine connections between heaven and earth. I realized that our prayers are tangible substance in God's eyes; He can see our prayers! He welcomes our words.

It was in 1959 when Malz suffered from a burst appendix and peritonitis. After weeks of suffering, her bodily functions stopped, and a nurse drew a sheet over her lifeless body. Immediately, Malz found herself in heaven. She writes:

> "Suddenly I was standing in the direct rays of radiant yellow light. I was erect and physically well. I saw powerful, direct shafts of light coming from the earth, directly to the throne room where the Great Light Source originates. I realized that these shafts were prayers ascending from the earth to the center of all creative power and merging with that Great Light."

Malz remembers wanting nothing more than to stay in that lovely place forever, but a powerful force was drawing her spirit back to earth—the power of prayer. "One prayer was meaningful to me," says Malz. "I saw it and heard it: '*JESUS*.' It was my father's voice. It asked for nothing, yet it asked for everything. In it was a wish, a desire, a plea; he wished I had not died. The name of Jesus drew me back, down the hill to the hospital room and back to my bed." Seconds later, Malz's own hand pushed the sheet off her face, as the life processes began functioning again in her body.

In her book, *Prayers That Are Answered,* Maltz tells this story:

"Grandma Rice discovered the power of the Name of Jesus when she was a young girl. She was walking across a field to pick blueberries when she stepped on a rotten, wooden cover of an open well. The boards snapped, and she pitched headlong into the dark water below. When she struck the water, she remembers feeling total panic. She couldn't swim or tread water. But she prayed one word *'JESUS!'* Nearby, a man was plowing a cornfield when he heard the words, "Turn off the motor." When he looked around, he saw no one and thought his mind was playing tricks on him. And then he heard the words again: *'Turn off the motor now!'* Just as he turned off the motor, he heard a splash and a muffled cry. He ran toward the sound, saw the well, grabbed an old rope lying by the well, and lowered it into the well. The young girl was choking and coughing, but she grabbed the rope and the man pulled her up." Yes, there is power in the name of Jesus!

The shafts of light rising to the heavens which Malz describes are indelibly tattooed in my mind. Often, in the midst of crisis, when my natural mind contains few rational words, the name of JESUS comes automatically, and as I speak that beautiful name, I know that shafts of light are traveling quickly to the throne room of heaven.

THE CIRCLE MAKER

> *Keep on asking and it will be given you, keep on seeking and you will find; keep on knocking and the door will be opened to you. For everyone who keeps on asking receives; and he who keeps on seeking finds; and to him who keeps on knocking, the door will be opened.*
> –Matthew 7:7-8

In his book, *The Circle Maker*, bestselling author Mark Batterson tells the story of Honi, a First Century sage, whose bold prayers ended a drought and saved a generation. Honi prayed: *"Lord of the universe, I swear before Your great name that I will not move from this circle until You have shown mercy upon Your children."* Honi stayed in the circle until the soaking, deluging, saturating rains came. Batterson reminds us that it was this kind of persistence that destroyed the walls of Jericho. It was

God's will that those walls be destroyed, but it had to be done along with the obedience of God's people as they marched around the city a prescribed number of times. "Jericho is spelled many different ways," writes Batterson. "If you have cancer, it's spelled healing. If your child is far from God, it's spelled salvation. If your marriage is falling apart, it's spelled reconciliation. If you have a vision beyond your resources, it's spelled provision." According to God's instructions, the Israelites circled Jericho seven times; after the seventh circle was completed, the walls fell. Quite often, those things which God wants for our lives must be circled with prayer over and over again. It is our persistence in prayer which pleases God.

To pray persistently does not mean that we are demanding our own way or seeking to satisfy selfish whims. Determined prayer must be based on what we believe to be God's will for our lives and the lives of others. We learn about God's will through a systematic reading of the Scriptures, and in so doing, we find the promises we can claim. "The transcript of our prayers becomes the transcript of your life," says Batterson. "Pray through the Bible. Think of scripture as God's part of the script; prayer is our part. Scripture is God's way of initiating a conversation; prayer is our response. The Bible was meant to be prayed through. Pray the Word. Pray the promises. The Holy Spirit will quicken certain promises to your spirit. God's word will not return void; He is watching over His Word to perform it."

In *The Circle Maker,* we are urged to pray circles around promises, miracles, dreams, and seemingly impossible situations. Batterson believes that the person you become is determined by how you pray. He says, "Ultimately, the transcript of your prayers becomes the script of your life." He believes that prayers never die because they are not subject to natural laws. He believes that his present life has been affected by prayers that his grandparents prayed for him years ago. He says that God's promises do not have expiration dates. "Praying is planting," says Batterson. "Each prayer is like a seed that gets planted in the ground. It disappears for a season, but it eventually bears fruit that blesses."

Pray Like Daniel

Then he said to me, "Do not fear, Daniel, for from the first day that you set your heart to understand, and to humble yourself before your God, your words were heard; and I have come because of your words."
—Daniel 10:12

In an article in *Mature Living* Magazine, Author Anne Graham Lotz says that Christians must learn to pray like Daniel. She explains that the Daniel way of praying is "a commitment that perseveres over any and every obstacle until heaven is moved and nations are changed. It's a commitment to pray until the prayer is answered." Daniel prayed three times a day. He had a special place in which to pray. He had a special time set aside for prayer. Daniel prayed even when his life was threatened.

"Daniel had a prepared attitude for prayer," says Anne Graham Lotz. "His body language—bowing his knees to God—helped him to remember that he, Daniel, a slave in exile, had an audience with the One who is the living God, All Glorious, Most Holy, the Ancient of Days, the Almighty. It was an outward gesture that revealed his inner attitude of humility, reverence, submission, and allegiance to the One so much greater than himself or any other earthly king or world ruler."

Daniel had a longing in his heart for his city and his people. He was determined to pray until the answer came. Daniel was not trying to change God's heart; rather, he was cooperating with God in bringing God's perfect will from heaven to earth. Satan tried to stop those prayers from being answered, but Daniel's persistence brought Heaven's power down to Earth.

Every Christian needs a special closet, a "War Room," where he shuts himself away from the distractions of the world and cries out to God in behalf of his family, his church, his nation and its leaders. In our prayer closet, we can pray earnest, heartfelt prayers, prayers that will change our world.

While our enemies may fight battles with angry words, Christians can fight battles on their knees, praying God's Word. We must go into our prayer closets daily and pray the Word of God. Yes, we can pray like Daniel with earnest, heartfelt intercession until Heaven is moved, and the will of God reigns.

The Prayer of Jabez

Jabez was honorable above his brothers, but his mother named him Jabez (sorrow maker), saying, Because I bore him in pain. Jabez cried to the God of Israel, saying, Oh, that You would bless me and enlarge my border, and that Your hand might be with me, and You would keep me from evil so it might not hurt me! And God granted his request.
1 Chronicles 4:9-10

Long before author Bruce Wilkinson wrote his best-selling book, *The Prayer of Jabez,* I found, amidst the endless begets in First Chronicles four, a character whom I could relate to. The way God answered that man's prayers gave me hope. The two verses about Jabez are like a mini novella, with a heart-rending story of hope. It occurred to me that if God had done that for Jabez, perhaps He would answer my prayers.

In a time when a name prophesied one's future, the mother of Jabez called her son a "sorrow maker," a child who caused her pain. Nevertheless, God described Jabez as a man who was "honorable" above his family members. Wilkerson tells us that Jabez prayed a "daring prayer that God always answers." In his book, Wilkinson encourages all Christians to reach for an extraordinary life, the life described in John 10:10: Jesus said, "I came that they may have and enjoy life, and have it in abundance (to the full, till it overflows.)"

Jabez was not making a selfish request of God. The "abundant" life is not a self-pampering existence. Rather, it is the life for which we were born to live, where you interact with other Christians using your God-given gifts and abilities to accomplish God's will on earth. As Wilkinson points out, when Jabez cried out to God, "Enlarge my territory!" he was looking at his present circumstances and concluded, "Surely, I was born for more than this!" We were each born for more than we can see with the physical eye. Wilkinson tells us, "God specializes in working through normal people who believe in a supernormal God who will do His work through them."

THE MAN WHO ASKED QUESTIONS

Call unto Me and I will answer you and show you great and mighty things, fenced in and hidden, which you do not know.
—*Jeremiah 33:3*

He has been described as the most remarkable American who ever lived. As child of slaves, George Washington Carver never knew his birth parents, and his name was never written on a birth certificate. As a young man, he traveled on foot for many miles in search of a school that would take a black student. In his travels, he came to the home of Mariah Watkins, a woman who had a simple, straightforward faith. She told George that God had a special plan for his life; she took him to church and introduced him to the wisdom of the Bible.

After failing to be accepted into several colleges because of his race, George Washington Carver was the first black man to be accepted at the University of Iowa. He became an artist, a musician, and an agricultural scientist, and served as President of the historically black Tuskegee University, in Tuskegee, Alabama.

When the boll weevil attacked the cotton crops and devastated the southern economy, Carver studied the problem and told the farmers to burn the cotton fields and then plant peanuts. Later, in the midst of a prolific peanut harvest, he prayed and asked for God's wisdom. "Mr.

Creator," he said, "why did you make the peanut?" In answer to his prayer, Carver eventually discovered over three hundred uses for the peanut. He developed a crop rotation that revolutionized agriculture. Henry Ford and Thomas Edison became his friends. Leaders from all over the world came to listen to his advice, as did three American presidents: Theodore Roosevelt, Calvin Coolidge, and Franklin Roosevelt. When Carver was asked about the source of his wisdom, he would often say, "God speaks to all of us each and every hour, if only we will listen. I silently ask the Creator, often moment by moment, to give me wisdom, understanding, and bodily strength to do His will. I am asking and receiving all the time." In answer to many prayers, the Creator gave Carver the knowledge to unlock many of nature's mysteries, and that knowledge was used in the service of others.

DEBBIE'S PERFECT WORD

The mightiest thing you can do for a man is to pray for him.
—T. Dewitt

Author Debbie Macomber's fictional books have been on every major bestseller list, and there are more than 140 million copies in print. However, it is her non-fiction stories that have enlarged my faith. In her book, *One Perfect Word,* there is a chapter on prayer in which she describes a time of trouble. "It was a pivotal year," she says. "Wayne and I were separated and completing all the legal requirements for our divorce. Our children were suffering. I was angry, lonely, and feeling like a failure." Nevertheless, in the midst of turmoil, she made a commitment to pray for one hour each day. Macomber would isolate herself and pray on her knees in her bedroom. "One hour is a very long time," she says. "Sixty slowly ticking minutes, and I don't even want to confess how many times my prayer in those first days was punctuated with requests for arthritic knee pain relief." Although her heart was heavy, she did not ask God to heal her marriage. Instead, she prayed that her husband would find happiness and peace and that he would be able to make a new life for himself without bitterness and animosity.

Macomber's prayer time was a season of relinquishment; she became willing for God to change her own life. As God began changing Debbie, her husband's heart was changing. Although it had been Wayne who had initially walked out of the marriage, he was the one to return and to suggest that they reunite and commit to a "forever" marriage. The Macombers have been married for more than forty years now.

As I retell this story, I wonder how many miracles would be available to each of God's children if we habitually shut ourselves inside a prayer closet and focused totally upon God's power, His strength, and His ability to do what we cannot do.

Prayer Prescription

Prayer is the way we write the future. It's the difference between letting things happen and making things happen.
–Mark Batterson

As I settle down on the mat with my head on a pillow and my right elbow positioned on a folded towel, Amy says, "Alright, Mrs. Dawkins, put your shoulder blades in your back pocket, hold them there, and slowly lift this weight. Do three sets of ten." My arm feels stiff and heavy as I lift the hand-weight thirty times. The next voice I hear is Dan's New York accent telling me it is time to work on the rowing machine; he has increased the weight, and I'm good to go.

I have been in physical therapy for two months now. Twice a week, I follow a series of exercises that my therapists designed for me. We are trying to strengthen my arm and shoulder blades which were damaged in an automobile accident. The process, a little painful at times, is not an instant fix, but a slow, tedious process. Nevertheless, it's a prescription for healing, and I am committed to following through with the plan my doctor has prescribed.

The Lord will often give me a prescription for receiving answers to serious prayer needs. He might impress me to pray three times daily about a particular need. He might lead me to fast and pray, or He may want me to enlist several friends to join me in prayer. I must follow through with the plan, even when circumstances seem worse, even when the slow, tedious process does not seem to be working, I must continue to pray. I will pray through; the answer is on the way.

Keeping Things Wound

We must daily keep things wound: that is, we must pray when prayer is dry as dust.
   ~Madeleine L'Engle, *Walking on Water*

In her book *Walking on Water,* Madeleine L'Engle tells this story:

In a small village, there was an old clockmaker who also repaired watches and clocks. When anything was wrong with the village people's timepieces, he was able to fix them. When the clockmaker died, having no children or apprentices, there was no one left to fix the clocks. Many of the clocks and watches began to break down, and the ones which continued to run lost time or gained time, so that they could not be trusted. Therefore, many of the villagers saw no use in continuing to wind their timepieces.

One day, a new clockmaker came to the village. After spending many hours tinkering with the watches and clocks, he finally announced that he could repair only those timepieces whose owners had kept them wound, because they were the only ones that would be able to remember how to keep time.

As Madeleine L'Engle tells this story, she advises, "We must daily keep things wound. That is, we must pray when prayer seems dry as dust. We may not always be able to make our 'clock' run correctly, but at least we can keep it wound so that it will not forget." L'Engle also says that serious writers form daily rituals. They exercise their writing muscles much like pianists play the scales. She says, "Inspiration does not always precede the act of writing; it often follows it." She would simply sit down and start to put words on paper each day, "most any words," she says. "Usually, then the words themselves will start to flow, they push me, rather than vice versa." In this way, she wrote many best-selling novels.

In the same way, our prayer lives will begin to thrive as we discipline ourselves to spend time each day communicating with the Lord.

Chapter Three

Life Saving Prayers

Sometimes the end of the rope is so near the surface of a person's soul. And we never know how one drop of rain might just push that person over the edge into the abyss. Yet one small prayer might be the difference that pulls them back from the brink.
— River Jordan, *Praying for Strangers*

Jerry's Prayer

For in You, O Lord, I hope; You will hear, O Lord my God.
—Psalm 38:15

My friend Jerry Bratu passed from this world to a better place a few years ago, but I can still hear his laughter and see the twinkle in his eyes as he told his stories. This is one of his true stories I won't forget:

Jerry was in the hospital, recovering from pneumonia when a cleaning lady came into his room. My friend, who seldom met a stranger he could not start a conversation with, began talking with the young woman who looked as though she might be pregnant.

They chatted, laughed, and made small-talk, while she tided his room. When she finished her work and started to leave, Jerry asked, "May I pray for you and your baby?" When she agreed, Jerry prayed, asking God to bless the woman's unborn child and to give the mother a healthy pregnancy and safe delivery. When he finished the prayer and looked up, he saw tears filling the woman's eyes. He then said, "Your baby is very special in God's sight. Did you know that?"

As tears continued to fall, the woman made a confession: she had planned to get an abortion. She then told Jerry that his prayer had created new thoughts in her mind. When she left the room, Jerry did not know what decision the lady would make. However, he had a peaceful feeling that he had obeyed a nudge from God, and he eventually forgot about it.

Years later, when he was shopping in Wal-Mart, a woman walked up, tapped him on the shoulder, and asked, "Sir, do you remember me? Fifteen years ago, you prayed for me, and I'm so glad you did." She then turned to the boy beside her and said, "This is my son. You told me he would be very special, and he is. He has blessed my life." When Jerry Bratu responded to a silent nudge and prayed with a stranger that day, a life was saved.

In her book, *One Perfect Word*, Debbie Macomber writes: "I get those nudges—like I ought to call someone I've wronged or I should take a casserole to a grieving family. I need to learn to recognize God's voice. The more we practice listening to His voice and acting on it, the better we get at recognizing it." Imagine how different this world could be if all of God's children were sensitive and obedient to His nudges!

Praying for Strangers

Prayer can change your world; it can change you; it can change your loved ones; it can change the larger world.
—Author Unknown

When author River Jordan's two sons were serving in Iraq and Afghanistan, her heart was heavy, and she desperately needed the prayers of other people. In an effort to get her mind off her own fears, she began reaching out to others, resolving to pray for at least one stranger each day. It could be the cashier at the grocery store, a man walking down the street, or a person on Facebook.

In her book, *Praying for Strangers,* Jordan explains that she was not an extremely outgoing person when it came to meeting strangers. At first, she felt foolish tapping someone on the shoulder and saying, "Excuse me, but today you're my stranger. I'll be praying special prayers all day for you." However, she found that most people were grateful, and most often they would tell her about their needs and give specific prayer requests.

She was easily drawn to people who looked helpless, such as the old man on the corner, the woman in ragged clothing, or the crumpled-over soul at the bus stop. But she found that well-dressed ladies driving expensive cars and wearing confident smiles often carried overwhelming, hidden burdens also.

While praying for strangers, Jordan became very sensitive to nudges from God. While driving down the street one day, she was impressed to knock on the door of a house which had a 'For-Sale' sign in the yard. When a tearful woman answered the door, Jordan knew she had found her stranger for the day. When she offered prayer, the woman confessed, "I planned to kill myself. I prayed one last prayer. I said, 'Lord, if you want me to live and not die today, just send someone to my door who will just listen to my story.'"

Tony Bellizzi, author of *The Fast Lane,* says that the list of secret pains of the people around us is endless and that every single person has a story. He believes that most people are seeking love, respect, and acceptance. He writes, "Opportunities to love are everywhere; just look around. Every school shooting you will hear about and every suicide you will ever know of is some person who might have been spared tragedy if they had been given a little kindness at some point in their lives." Bellizzi suggests that we educate ourselves about what's going on in our world, and he cites these facts:

One in four babies are murdered by abortion. One in one hundred Americans are in jail. Forty percent of American teens self-mutilate. One in one hundred teens have an eating disorder. Slavery and human trafficking are thriving in America.

River Jordan and Toni Bellizzi remind us that we live in a destitute world filled with needy people of all descriptions and that we are very important to each other. Jordan ends her story with: "Sometimes the end of the rope is so near the surface of a person's soul. And we never know how one more drop of rain might just push that person over the edge into the abyss. Yet one small prayer might be the difference that pulls them back from the brink."

Street Prayers

The effective, fervent prayer of a righteous man avails much.
—James 5:16

I have been encouraged by the true prayer stories in author Ronald Dunn's book, *Don't Just Stand There, Pray Something.* My favorite story in the book is about the lady who had to leave her sick child at home in order to get his prescription filled at the pharmacy. After she purchased the medication and returned to her car, she realized her keys were locked inside. She desperately needed to get back to her child, and time was precious. Right there, with her eyes wide open, she stood on the street and began praying. Immediately, an old dented car rattled up and stopped. A young man got out and offered help. After she explained the problem, he took a rusted coat-hanger, and with a couple of skillful moves opened her car door. Overcome with gratitude, she profusely thanked the man, "You are an answer to prayer, young man. You must be a Christian."

"No ma'am," he replied, "I'm not a Christian, and I'm not a good boy. I just got out of prison yesterday." The lady's smile never faded as she exclaimed, "Well, how about that, God sent me a professional!" It isn't always necessary to get on your knees or to go inside a church to have your prayers answered. Eyes-wide-open street prayers can be very effective.

Sometimes, God even dispatches angels when people are bold enough to pray in public. Our friend Gary Weatherford once stopped on a street corner where a child had been hit by a car. He remembers joining with a tall, dark-skin man to intercede for the little girl while emergency help was on the way. As soon as the child was safely in the ambulance, Gary turned to speak again to the man who had prayed with him. Strangely, the man had disappeared. Gary later learned that those street-prayers had been effective, and he wondered if God had supplied an angel for his prayer partner that day.

Street corner prayers are needed daily. I believe God is looking down for willing intercessors to intervene on behalf of His children. When an ambulance, a firetruck, or a police car zooms by with siren blaring, someone is in need of prayer. When I pull over for the emergency vehicle to pass, I can begin praying with eyes wide open for people I do not know. Having been involved in an automobile accident, some time ago, I have empathy for people in similar circumstances, and I see more clearly the need for spontaneous street prayers. I will never forget what it feels like to be helplessly trapped inside a wrecked car on the side of the highway at midnight. One word came to my muddled brain, and I whispered it over and over again: "JESUS! JESUS! JESUS!" God brought immediate help to my family and me—medical students who stayed with us until the ambulances came.

God works in this world according to the prayers of ordinary people like you and me, so, don't just stand there; pray something!

The Choice

Before I formed you in your mother's womb, I knew you.
-Jeremiah 1:5

Beth Sharp, Director of the Center for Pregnancy Choices, believes that every child is a gift from God. However, she did not always see it that way. There was a time when an unplanned pregnancy seemed only to be an interruption of her life plans. When she was seventeen, she had an abortion. A decade later, she was certain that abortion was the answer again, so she made an appointment.

When Beth's friends learned of the appointment with the abortion clinic, they began praying earnestly that Beth would change her mind. Nevertheless, she soon made her way to the abortion clinic alone. When she was prepped, lying on the table, and waiting for the procedure, an unbelievable thing happened. The doctor walked in and said, "I'm sorry, but I can't do this. I cannot perform an abortion for you."

Today, she knows that it was the prayers of her friends and the pleas of her praying grandmother that intervened and saved the life of her baby girl. Later, when she saw the sonogram and the tiny beating heart, she grieved at the thought of what might have been. A miracle happened that day; a life was saved, and the life of the mother was forever changed.

Today she tells her story wherever she goes. "All I have is a voice," says Beth, "and I am compelled to tell my story to women everywhere." Now she knows that it is actually God's hand that forms each baby in its mother's womb, and her key scripture is: "Before I made you in your mother's womb, I knew you" (Jeremiah 1:5). When Beth speaks in schools and civic organizations, her beautiful daughter often goes with her. Sometimes the question is asked of the daughter, "How does it make you feel that your mother didn't want you?" She answers, "The important thing is that God wanted me."

As the director of the Center for Pregnancy Choices, Beth and her staff offer 24-hour counseling, free pregnancy tests, post-abortion counseling, and referrals for adoption, medical assistance, employment, and education. All visits are free and confidential. Beth believes there is a great need for post-abortion healing, and she says, "Women need to heal after abortion in order to forgive themselves of the shame and guilt. They need a revelation that after repentance, God remembers their sins no more. Also, talking about it with a group brings peace. Knowing there are others that made that choice too makes it easier to release. And last, knowing that the child went straight into the arms of Jesus brings happiness and one day there will be a great reunion."

Don't Ever Give Up!

The thief does not come except to steal, and to kill, and to destroy. I have come that they may have life and that they may have it more abundantly.
—John 10:10

My friend, Anne, advises people with incurable diseases and impossible problems: "Don't ever give up!" She was a victim of an incurable illness that stole four and a half years of her life and threatened her sanity. She knows what it means to be a born-again, spirit-filled Christian, yet have your faith dwindle to nothing and to be completely dependent on other people's prayers.

The tool that Satan used in an attempt to ravage her faith is called Multiple Chemical Sensitivity. Victims of this misunderstood illness are highly susceptible to adverse effects from a wide range of household and industrial chemicals, such as cleaning products, tobacco smoke, perfumes, inks, pesticides, and plastics, as well as certain foods.

When exposed to such things, Anne's body reacted with headaches, nausea, dizziness, fatigue, hair-loss, respiratory difficulties, and extreme depression. She often felt as though a searing hot poked was lodged inside her chest. Depression ruled her mind; she believed that she and her entire family would eventually die of chemical exposure.

After seeking help in churches and treatment facilities, she saw no change and became completely hopeless. "My mind became emptier and emptier," Anne recalls, "I couldn't sleep at night. I desperately sought distraction from my 'hell on earth.' Television became my mind pacifier." So, for four and a half years she lay on the couch, watching television and waiting to die.

Anne is a new person today. She came back to life the day after hurricane Katrina swept through her hometown. It was as though some of her symptoms had blown away with the storm. Her mind became peaceful, and she realized God's healing was at work in her body and mind.

Although it was not an instant miracle, Anne believes that God's healing came to her in a slow release process, as a direct result of the cumulative prayers of Meridian's Christian community. "There are times when a person cannot muster up the faith it takes for healing," Anne says. "That's when other people must come to their aid. So, if you are praying for someone who is unable to pray for themselves, keep on praying. Don't ever give up!"

The Teacher Who Learned to Pray

When one learns to find God, all fear is dispelled; and finding God is entirely a matter of prayer, a simple request that God, who Himself has said that He is within you, reveal Himself to you.
—Margaret Madden

This true story comes from the book *Your Prayers are Always Answered*, written by Alexander Lake. The setting is a small California cow town with dusty streets, in the year 1919. It is an example of the power of small prayers that can cause a ripple effect throughout the cities and towns in which we live.

When a teacher, newly graduated from college, arrived in town from her first assignment, she found streets ankle-deep in dust, broken wooden sidewalks, unpainted houses, and shabby stores with ugly false-fronts. Even the church on the corner wore an air of discouragement.

When she walked into her classroom, Margaret Madden's heart sank to a new low. "The students were in keeping with the rest of the town—unkept, dressed in patched, faded, soiled clothes," said Margaret Madden. "There was resentment and dislike in the eyes that stared at me. Only one little girl had a friendly smile. Her name was Myrtle." Classes did not go well; the students were often tardy and failed to do homework assignments. The children were not learning, and Margaret feared she would lose her job.

One day, Myrtle's grandmother came to visit the teacher, bringing a bouquet of flowers, a red-letter New Testament, and these encouraging words: "Myrtle has told me about you, Miss Madden, and she prays for you every night. You are a fine young woman, and God needs you to do great things in this town of ours. The children you are teaching now are our hope for the future. You can help them so much. You can inspire this whole town."

When Myrtle's grandmother left, Miss Madden thought about the only child who smiled in the classroom and always did her homework—the child that was on her knees every night, praying for her teacher.

The teacher opened her new Bible and read words that the grandmother had marked: "Your Father knoweth what things ye have need of... Ask and it shall be given you; seek, and ye shall find; knock and it shall be opened unto you... Take heed that you do not despise one of these little ones... Feed My lambs." And then the teacher began to pray.

The next day in class, Miss Madden and her students began talking about the problems in the classroom and the problems of their town. And that is how it all began. Within a week, they worked out their start of a project. George, who had artistic abilities that no one had known about, drew a sketch of his own house. There were no trees or shrubs on the lawn, and the house looked boxy and plain. On another sheet of paper, he drew the house he wished to live in—a wide front porch, a low shallow-roofed wing on one side, a trellised portico on the other side. Other students offered suggestions for paint colors and shrubbery placement. This was the first project which led to other people improving their own properties across the town. Furthermore, various phases of the first renovation project required that the class study fascinating by-way projects. "For instance," said the teacher, "reading about shingles took us to cedar forests. Cement led us to lime, and lime to rock formations."

Later, Dr. Clarke Robinson, a San Francisco educator, wrote regarding Miss Madden: "Prayer enabled Miss Madden to innovate her projects thirty years before that method was accepted as the latest concept in education. She discovered her students' aptitudes, and put them to work on matters affecting everyday life. Miss Madden taught her pupils also the importance of each person in the scheme of things. We need teachers who pray."

Chapter Four

Prayers That Never Die

I had a grandfather who would kneel by his bedside every night, take off his hearing aids, and pray for his family. He couldn't hear himself without his hearing aids, but everyone else in the house could. He died when I was six, but sometimes I hear a whisper in my spirit, "Mark, the prayers of your grandfather are being answered in your life right now."
—Mark Batterson, *The Circle Maker*

Monica's Prayers

The king's heart is in the hand of the Lord, like the rivers of water; He turns it wherever He wishes.
-Proverbs 21:1

Perhaps she breathed her first prayer when she felt a tiny butterfly flutter inside her stomach—so slight that she might have imagined it. And maybe she stood perfectly still and held her breath just to be sure. With the second movement, she knew it was real. Her baby had moved!

How could she explain the joy—the incredible love she felt for the tiny child inside her womb? I am sure she prayed and spent days planning how to be the perfect mother and raise a perfect child. She would create a safe haven and teach him all the right things. She was determined that this child would become better than his parents had ever had a chance to be.

When he was born, it was the happiest day of her life. She held him in her arms and thanked God for her greatest blessing.

His childhood passed quickly—like pages blowing in the wind. He took his first steps, spoke his first words, and began discovering the world around him. All too soon, he was no longer a baby, but a unique personality with thoughts of his own. Every day, she prayed and taught him God's Word.

The boy child became a man with a brilliant, willful mind of his own, and he left the protection of his mother's arms to go out into the world. Now, Monica prayed more than ever, sometimes with fear, sometimes with faith, but always with hope that God would do what she could no longer do.

Nevertheless, while the prayers collected in heaven, the prodigal son took a mistress, fathered an illegitimate child, and then joined a cult. Monica's heart was broken. How could it be that a child taught of the Lord from birth could so rebelliously blaspheme His Name? Yet, while Monica grieved, her prayers never stopped.

One night, she had a dream. She was walking hand-in-hand with her son on the streets of heaven. She woke knowing that this was a message of encouragement from God. Although she believed that the miracle would come quickly, she saw no immediate change. She prayed diligently for nine long years.

Finally, in desperation, Monica went to a church official and begged him to reason with her wayward son. The man replied, "Go home, and continue your prayers. It is not possible that the son of such tears should be lost!" With those words, she was encouraged once more.

Perhaps, it was when a sufficient number of prayers accumulated at the Heavenly throne, God spoke. The prodigal son heard a voice: "Take up and read. Take up and read." Aurelius heard those words and looked up, searching for the voice. He heard only a group of children in a nearby field and thought how strange that children would chant such a thing. Suddenly, he realized a Heavenly voice commanding him to take up the Bible and read. He obeyed, and his heart was changed forever.

It had taken twenty-nine years of constant intercession to bring forth the man the world would come to know as Saint Augustine. Monica never knew the extent of God's plan for her son's life—that later it would be said that the course of history was changed because Saint Augustine lived, spoke, and wrote as a champion of the Christian faith.

Sonya's Prayers

And your ears will hear a word behind you, saying, this is the way, walk in it.
-—Isaiah 30:21

Sonya remembers shuffling from one foster care home to another and being ignored or laughed at because she was different from other children. When she was thirteen, she met and married a handsome man who promised to make her life happy and exciting. Though the promise was never fulfilled, the two little boys resulting from the marriage became the most important part of her life.

When Ben and Curtis were seven and nine, their father left home and never returned. Life became a constant struggle for Sonya, who had only a third-grade education and no earning skills. She could see no hope for a decent life for her children. Eventually, because of physical problems and extreme depression, she was confined to a mental hospital.

While in the hospital, her life turned around when someone taught Sonya how to read the Bible and pray. As her faith grew stronger, she cried out to God, "Lord, if You can take nothing and make the world out of it, You can take my situation and make it work for my boys' sake. My boys need help and they deserve a chance."

With this plea, Sonya began a daily conversation with God. "I would pray for guidance," she said, "and afterward I would know what to do—there was not so much a voice as a certainty, a feeling of what to say or do."

When Curtis and Ben brought home report cards with failing grades, their mother talked with God about it. And then she got the idea to restrict their TV watching to only two programs a week; instead of watching television, they were to read two books from the library per week and write a book report on each. Although Curtis and Ben complained about such restrictions, Sonya explained, "I asked God for wisdom, and this is what I got." The boys began reading and writing book reports. Eventually, their grades improved.

Sonya taught her boys the importance of their own personal choices, saying, "The person who has the most to do with what happens to you is you! You make the choices; you decide whether you are going to give up when the going gets tough. Ultimately, it is you who decides whether you will be a success, or not by doing what is legally necessary to get you where you want to go. You are the captain of your own ship. If you don't succeed, you only have yourself to blame."

Because of a mother who guided her children toward faith in God and confidence in themselves, Curtis and Ben escaped a nearly illiterate, inner-city neighborhood. Curtis became a successful aeronautical engineer. Ben became Dr. Benjamin Carson, head of pediatric neurosurgery at Johns Hopkins Hospital, and he is known across the world as the first surgeon to successfully separate conjoined twins who were joined at the head.

Victor's Mother

Ask, and it will be given you; seek and you will find.
—Matthew 7:7

In the 1960s, a young mother moved her family from Puerto Rico to New York City, in search of a better life. However, their New York neighborhood was riddled with all kinds of drugs and violence. Victor was only twelve when a gang recruited him. By the time he was fourteen, he was hooked on heroin and had been arrested for stealing and mugging.

The mother was heartbroken. She was a small woman, who spoke no English. But there was one thing she knew how to do, and that was to pray. Every day, seven days a week and twice on Sundays, she would go early in the morning to a little storefront church with her sister, where they would pray together for Victor. Victor's mother did not just pray that God would protect her son, keep him out of trouble, and set him free from drugs; she also asked God to make her son a minister and to use him to bring other young men to the Lord.

When Victor continued to take drugs and often came home at three in the morning, high and out-of-control, his mother would hug him and say, "Victor, God's hand is on you, and He has a calling on your life. He's saving you and making you a minister."

However, it seemed that the more she prayed the worse Victor acted. His teacher at school told her, "Your son is going to end up in the electric chair! I've never seen anyone so out of control."

Even though there was no sign of improvement, the mother continued praying, month after month. What she could not see was that God was working, preparing a man by the name of David Wilkerson, who lived in another state, to come and minister on the roughest streets of New York.

Eventually, the out-of-control young man heard David Wilkerson preaching on a street corner. Victor responded to the message. He knelt down and gave his life to Christ. God set him free from heroin, brought him out of the gang, and removed him from a life of violence. Victor eventually became pastor of a great church, New Life Outreach, in Richmond, Virginia. He also traveled all over the world telling his story to drug addicts.

A Father's Prayers

The effective, fervent prayer of a righteous man avails much.
—James 5:16

In author Catherine Marshall's book, *Beyond Ourselves,* there is the story of Starr Daily. When Starr was sixteen years old, his only ambition had been to build a reputation as a dangerous man. He dreamed of the time when the police would refer to him with a shudder. He achieved this aim by becoming the leader of a gang of safecrackers. There was no safe he could not open. But finally, liquor made him careless and he was caught. In 1924, he was sentenced to a major prison for the third time. There followed fourteen years of penal farms, chain gangs, and two extended penitentiary sentences. Through all that time, Starr's father never lost hope that his son might be redeemed from his life of crime. The broken-hearted man died with a prayer for his son on his lips.

In prison, Starr made two futile attempts to escape. Then he evolved a plan to instigate a prison riot. The deputy warden was to be seized and used as a shield and hostage. The plan failed, and Starr was sentenced to the dungeon.

In those day, American prisons were often brutal places. Most strong men could not survive the dungeon for more than fifteen days. It was winter, and the walls of the dank cell seeped moisture. At six every morning, the prisoner would be given a piece of bread and a cup of water. Then he would be lifted to hang in handcuffs for twelve hours. At six in the evening, he would be let down for the night and given another piece of bread and another cup of water.

Starr survived fifteen days of this, but by the last day in the cuffs, he could no longer stand on his feet, black with congealed blood. The keeper of the dungeon had to lift the almost-unconscious man into the cuffs. For weeks after that, the prisoner was allowed to lie on the icy stone floor-emaciated, filthy, and near death. Mired in the lowest hell imaginable, only hate was keeping him alive— hate for the deputy warden.

Then there came a moment when the man on the floor was too weak to hate. He knew he was dying. There followed a half-waking, half-sleeping state of unconsciousness, moments of delirium, and times of awareness. This was followed by disconnected dreams, like mists floating across the brain. The prisoner was no longer aware of the frozen stone floor, of his filth, or of anyone who came or went. Finally, the dreams began to take on meaning.

Suddenly, Starr seemed to be in a garden. Jesus Christ, the Man whom he had been trying to avoid all his life, was coming toward him. Jesus stood face-to-face with Starr, looking deep into his eyes as if penetrating the bottom of his soul. Love of a quality that he had never felt before was drawing the hate out of his heart; it was like extracting poison from an infected wound. Starr began to think, *"I'll never be the same again, now and through all eternity."*

There followed another dream in which all the people Starr had ever injured passed before his eyes. One by one, he poured out his love to them. Then all who had injured him appeared, and on them, too, he bestowed the love needed to restore and to heal. The love flowed from beyond him, poured through him in a torrent of caring and ecstatic gratitude.

When the prisoner returned to consciousness, the cell did not look the same. Its grim grayness was gone. For him, it was illuminated with a warm light. His feelings, too, were different. The prison environment no longer had the power to give him pain, only joy.

Through a swift, surprising series of events, prison doors swung open for Starr Daily. He left prison five years ahead of the time set for his release. The man who had been considered a hopeless criminal had been cured of all criminal tendencies.

In 1961, Catherine Marshall wrote, "From this man, who had only a sixth-grade education, have come eight books. He has lectured all over the nation. His knowledge of the criminal mind has contributed to valuable rethinking of prison techniques. He has personally been the Holy Spirit's vehicle for the reclamation of scores of criminals."

Starr Daily said, "The Holy Spirit came to me through the glorified Christ. He did not give me the gifts of the Spirit, rather the fruits of the spirit to be worked out in a day to day discipline. Perhaps that was necessary in my case, so that the fruits could be integrated with the drastic character changes necessary."

Chapter Five

Impossible Things

For with God nothing will be impossible.
—Luke 1:37

BROOKLYN TABERNACLE CHURCH

When prayer comes from a sincere heart, it rises into God's presence and stays there. The more prayers you add, the more they collect in heaven. They do not evaporate like gas. They remain before God.
—Jim Cymbala

In 1971, Jim Cymbala and his wife, Carol, began their ministry at Brooklyn Tabernacle Church, in New York City. The building was shabby. The basement reeked with mildew; the ceiling in the auditorium fell with a huge thud during a service one day, and a pew full of people collapsed in the sanctuary on a Sunday morning. Church attendance had dwindled to less than thirty people, and the church's checking account held approximately ten dollars. Alcohol and heroin dominated the neighborhood, and prostitutes were working the nearby streets.

Years earlier, a group of ladies had formed a prayer group and asked God to establish a congregation in downtown Brooklyn that would touch people for God's glory. That was the way Brooklyn Tabernacle began. When its future seemed hopeless, Jim Cymbala prayed a broken prayer: "Lord, I have no idea how to be a successful pastor. I haven't trained. All I know is that Carol and I are working in the middle of New York City with people dying on every side, overdosing from heroin, consumed by materialism, and all the rest…"

In the middle of an unfinished prayer, deep within his spirit, the weeping minister sensed God speaking. *If you and your wife will lead my people to pray and call upon my name, you will never lack for something fresh to preach, I will supply all the money that's needed, both for the church and for your family, and you will never have a building large enough to contain the crowds I will send in response.*

Later, Jim Cymbala told his congregation, "From this day on, the prayer meeting will be the barometer of our church. What happens on Tuesday night will be the gauge by which we will judge success or failure because that will be the measure by which God blesses us. Prayer is the engine that will drive the church."

As people prayed, God responded. The pastor began preaching anointed sermons, while his wife played the piano and gathered a group of singers for the choir. "We never knew who might come to Christ at Brooklyn Tabernacle," says Jim Cymbala. "There were junkies, prostitutes, lost lawyers, business types, and bus drivers who turned to the Lord there. We welcomed them all."

Slowly, the little church with the big problems was transformed into a spiritual emergency room. "It became a place of rescue," said Carol Cymbala, "for those who felt crushed by the darkness around them, by the violence, addiction, harshness, and despair that characterized the city. God's medicine began to work wonders."

The choir began with nine people and would later grow to Two hundred and seventy-five members. Carol explains that they realized early on that their job was not to perform but to lead people into the presence of God. As they worshipped, people were drawn into their fellowship.

When asked about the success of the Brooklyn Tabernacle Choir, Carol responded, "How likely is it that someone who barely made it through high school and who can't even read a note of music would ever stand on the stage of Radio City Music Hall or Carnegie Hall? How likely is it that the choir would win four Grammy awards and record twenty albums?"

Winters in New York can be brutal and convenient parking spaces are few; people who drive to church often have to park eight to ten blocks away, and taxis, vans, and charter buses bring groups of visitors from far away places. Sometimes on New Year's Eve people line up for hours, waiting outside in frigid temperatures to get inside the Brooklyn Tabernacle Church.

Brooklyn Tabernacle now has a larger building and 16,000 members. It is one of the biggest churches in the Greater New York area. Is it the music, the preaching, or some clever program that draws people there? Jim and Carol Cymbala give all credit to God the Creator, who arranged all in response to prayer.

Heaven Is For Real

Jesus came to get me. He said I had to go back because He was answering your prayer.
—Colton Burpo

When three-year-old Colton Burpo suffered a burst appendix and lay near death on the operating table, his father raged at God. "You're going to take my son? Why are you taking my son away?" God overlooked the young pastor's angry words and miraculously healed Colton.

Months later, in a casual conversation, Colton remarked, "The angels sang to me and I sat in Jesus' lap." Todd Burpo thought perhaps his son had dreamed about Jesus and the angels, but in the months that followed, the little boy described his visit to heaven, and Todd realized that what his son described was indeed very real.

"I went up out of my body," Colton said. "When I was with Jesus, I looked down and I could see the doctor working on my body, and you were in a little room on your knees, and mommy was praying and talking on the phone. You needed the Holy Spirit, so I was praying for you."

Over the next three years, the little boy continued talking about Heaven, what he had seen and the people he had met there. Colton described Heaven as a place that needs no lights, because God and Jesus light up Heaven. He saw many children there, and one of them was his sister. Colton was surprised because he had never been told about his mother's miscarriage. He met his grandfather who had died decades before Colton's birth. He said he also met Jesus' cousin whose name is John. He described Jesus, who was wearing a white robe with a purple sash, and he remarked, "Oh, Dad, his eyes are so pretty!" The Burpos searched through many pictures of Jesus, and with each rendering they would ask Colton, "Does this look like Jesus?" Each time, Colton would say, "No. That's not right."

Eventually, the Burpos learned about a CNN report featuring a young Lithuanian American girl named Akiane Kramarik. The CNN segment, described twelve-year-old, Akiane, as a child prodigy, a self-taught artist. Although she had had no spiritual training, she was not familiar with the Bible, as her mother was an atheist, she began having visions of heaven at the age of four. She described Jesus in a similar way as Colton had, "He's big and strong, and He has the most beautiful eyes." Colton's dad watched the CNN report, recorded it, and immediately called Colton in to view it. When Colton saw the portrait of Jesus which Akiane had painted, he stood staring at the rendering of Jesus, and then said, "Dad, that one's right!"

Little Colton told his dad that God shoots down power to us when someone prays. "It's the Holy Spirit," Colton said. "I watched Him. He showed me. He shoots down power for you when you're talking in church." Todd recalled that every Sunday morning he would pray, "God, if you don't help this morning, this message is going to fail." That humble prayer had literally brought God's power down from Heaven into a needy world.

To Heaven And Back

If two of you agree about anything you ask for, it will be done for you by my Father in heaven. For where two or three come together in my name, there I am with them.
—Matthew 18:19-20

In 1999, in the Los Rios region of Southern Chile, orthopedic surgeon Dr. Mary Neal drowned in a kayak accident. While cascading down a waterfall, her kayak became pinned at the bottom, and she was immediately and completely submerged. Despite the rescue efforts of her companions, Mary was underwater far too long.

"When I first realized that I was pinned in the waterfall," writes Mary, "I did not panic and I did not struggle, but I desperately tried to get out of my boat. I tried to push against the foot braces. I tried to jiggle the boat. I thought about my family and desperately tried to raise my head out of the water in search of air. I quickly realized that I was not in control of my future."

However, God had intervened in Mary's life more than once, so once again, she reached out to Him. She says, "I did not demand rescue. I knew that He loved me and had a plan for me. I asked only that His will be done."

While her body was being slowly sucked out of the boat, she felt as though her soul was slowly peeling itself away from her body. "I rose up and out of the river, and when my soul broke through the surface of the water, I encountered a group of fifteen to twenty souls who greeted me with the most overwhelming joy," says Mary. "They were sort of like a large welcoming committee." Mary believes that those who met her were sent to guide her across the divide of time and dimension that separates our world from God's.

Her arrival in Heaven was joyously celebrated, and she seemed to be surrounded by love. Mary says, "We hugged and danced and greeted each other. It was as though I was experiencing an explosion of love and joy." But as she was drinking in the beauty and rejoicing with her companions, she glanced back at the scene on the river bank. "My body looked like the shell of a comfortable old friend."

She saw her friends on the river bank performing CPR, and she could hear them begging her to take a breath. It was their prayers and their sadness that drew her back. She says, "I loved them and did not want them to be sad, so I asked my heavenly companions to wait while I returned to my body, and took a breath."

However, on returning to her damaged body, Mary suffered multiple injuries, advanced pneumonia and acute respiratory distress that often leads to death. On reaching the hospital, her internist gravely told her husband that she would probably not make it through the night. On hearing this news, more friends began praying. They prayed that God would save her life and heal her body. They prayed intensely, passionately, and specifically. One friend went home and continued to pray until four in the morning, when suddenly she felt like she could rest. "For much of the night, my body struggled for survival," says Mary. "According to the medical records, about 4:00 a.m., the same time Natalie felt released from prayer, my vital signs stabilized. I was going to make it after all."

The Last Survivor of Nine Eleven

Is any one of you in trouble? He should pray.
~James 5:13

Jim Cymbala tells the story of the last survivor of the Nine-Eleven tragedy in his book, *Break Through Prayer.*

Genelle Guzman-McMillan grew up on the Caribbean Island of Trinidad. Though her mother was a devout Catholic, Genelle didn't like church, thinking it was a waste of time. She left Trinidad and moved to New York City in 1998, where she gained employment as an office worker on the sixty-fourth floor of the North Tower of the World Trade Center.

On the morning of September 11, as she was making small talk with a co-worker, suddenly the building began to shake. Someone shouted that a plane had hit the building. What followed was a time of confusion. Not realizing what had actually happened, Genelle and her co-worker could not decide if they should remain in the office or head for the elevator. When they finally headed out, they discovered the elevators were no longer working, and someone had reported smoke on the stairs.

When the second plane hit the South Tower, the building began swaying and rocking. Genelle was sure they were going to die. She and her co-worker, Rosa, held hands, and crying and shaking, they joined a group of people heading down the stairway. By the time they reached the thirteenth floor, "The whole place just went boom!" says Genelle. "Rosa and I fell back toward the wall, and then I fell to the floor. Everything was crumbling around us. It was pitch black. My eyes and mouth were filled with grit and dust. One hundred ten floors were coming down around us. I knew I was being buried alive." Genelle lay on her right side, with her right leg pinned beneath something heavy. When she tried to move her head, she found that her hair, done up in cornrows, was pinned under the concrete. When she started calling for Rosa, there was no response. Trapped in dark silence, Genelle began thinking of her children, her family, and her fiancé, she wondered what would happen to her after she died. She did not know how to ask for forgiveness, and she was sure she was headed for Hell.

She was in and out of consciousness, and every time she woke up, she tried removing the rubble with her left hand, the only part of her that could move freely, but made no progress. Her head was starting to swell. Helplessly, she started to pray, "God, I can't take this pain. Help me get my head free of the concrete." Then she made one hard pull, yanking upwards. She could feel the cornrows ripping from her scalp. Her head was bleeding, but at least, she was free.

Genelle felt iron and steel sticking into her side. She tried to remove the rubble, but it was too heavy and hard. She slept again, and when she woke, she prayed, "God, you've got to help me! You've got to show me a sign, show me a miracle, give me a second chance, and I promise I will do Your will. Please save my life!"

The next day she heard a beep-beep sound like a truck backing up. She called for help, but there was no response. She called out again. Finally, someone hollered back, "Hello, is somebody there?" She stretched out her hand, but the rescue workers could not see it. She lost consciousness. When she woke, she stretched out her hand as far as she could, and this time someone took her hand and held it. A voice said, "Genelle, I've got you, you're going to be alright. My name is Paul. I won't let go of your hand until they get you out."

"As soon as he grabbed my hand, I felt complete calmness throughout my body," said Genelle. "Paul kept telling me I would be alright. I kept his name in my head, because I wanted to meet him when I got out and thank him."

The rescue workers reached her, put her on a stretcher and passed her hand to hand up and down a long line of people. When the sunlight finally hit her face, everyone was clapping. It had been twenty-seven hours since the towers collapsed. Genelle was the last survivor to be pulled out of the wreckage of what had once been the World Trade Towers.

When she inquired about a man named Paul, she was told there was no one on the rescue team by that name. She told her story on *Oprah* and CNN on television, and in *Guidepost* and *Time* magazines. Still, no one named Paul stepped forward to take credit for rescuing Genelle.

The Rest of Paul's Story

Eventually, with the help of journalist William Croyle, Genelle wrote *Angel in the Rubble.* Not long after this book was published, the mystery of Paul was solved. William Croyle received a phone call from a New York Fire-fighter who said, "My name is Paul Somin; I wanted you to know that I am real." The mysterious Paul was not an angel as Genelle had believed. He was actually a New York firefighter who had wished to remain anonymous. However, Genelle still believes that the man who held her hand for at least twenty minutes while the rescue workers struggled to reach her was God's miracle. He was a messenger of God's love in the midst of pain.

GOD WANTS TO DO IMPOSSIBLE THINGS

Be anxious for nothing, but in everything by prayer and supplication, with thanksgiving, let your requests be made known to God.
—Philippians 4:6

The question is often asked? If God is sovereign, why does He need our prayers? Chinese Theologian Watchman Nee asked that question and wrote a book called *Let Us Pray.* He says, "We know that God never does anything against His own will. But, do we not see that prayer is the asking of God to fulfill HIS needs? The prayers of believers are to accomplish God's will." Nee demonstrates this truth by sharing a parable: "Prayer is the rail for God's work. Indeed, prayer is to God's will as rails are to a train. The locomotive is full of power; it is capable to running a thousand miles a day. But if there are no rails, it cannot move forward a single inch. If it dares to move without them, it will soon sink into the earth. It cannot go to anyplace where no rails have been laid."

God has chosen to involve His people in bringing about His will on earth. "However," says Nee, "Satan will rise up to hinder such prayer. All prayers which come from God touch the powers of darkness." Daniel prayed for twenty-one days, and then Gabriel came to tell him: "Do not fear Daniel, for from the first day that you set your heart to understand, and to humble yourself before your God, your words were heard; and I have come because of your words. But the prince of the Kingdom of Persia withstood me twenty-one days" (Daniel 10:12-13).

There is a battle in the Heavens. Therefore, if we do not take up the responsibility of prayer, we will hinder the fulfillment of God's will. God gave His children freewill. Nee reminds us that there are three wills, the will of God, the will of Satan, and the will of man. "God seeks to have our wills joined with His," says Nee. He will not destroy Satan's will all by Himself. When the Lord wishes to do a thing, He first puts His own thought in us through the Holy Spirit. Only after we have turned this thought into prayer will He perform it."

Chapter Six

Journaling

Next to my Bible, nothing is more sacred to me than my journal. It's the way I mark my trail. It's the way I process problems and record revelations. It's the way I keep track of the prayers I've prayed so that I can give God the glory when He answers.
    –Mark Batterson, *Draw the Circle*

CHANGE YOUR LIFE

We have a loving, powerful God who listens to us with pleasure, and longs to guide us into a life that is beautiful, good, and true.
    –Winn Collier

Successful author and life coach Becky Tirabassi was once an out of control, overweight, alcoholic. And then she cried out to God for help. As a result, she discovered a life-changing secret: The practice of spending the first hour of every day conversing with God will change your life.

She describes herself as a rebellious, beer-drinking, disco-dancing, smart-mouthed teenager, who moved on to drugs, binge drinking, and living with boyfriends. "By the time I was twenty-one," says Tirabassi, "I had fallen to a point of personal destruction. I woke one morning in bed next to a man I barely knew. I was humiliated that I had no recollection of what I had done with him the night before."

Faced with the truth that she actually was an alcoholic, she was overwhelmed with fear and hopelessness. Knowing that she needed something or someone to take control of her life, she drove to the nearest church to look for a pastor. Although she never found the pastor, the church janitor found Tirabassi crying in the basement hall. He listened to her story and led her to the Lord. "Through a simple, but incredibly transparent and powerful prayer with the janitor of the church," says Tirabassi, "I found God waiting for me." However, the sinner's prayer was only the beginning for Tirabassi. She then began seeking a daily relationship with the Lord that would lead to a complete lifestyle change.

She writes her prayers in a journal, confessing her sins and spelling out her frustrations and struggles in honest words. In this way, she is speaking to God. When she opens her Bible, God speaks to her, and she records those scriptures in her journal. In her daily appointment with God, she also discusses ideas, dreams, and goals, and makes plans for each day.

In Tirabassi's workbook, *Let Prayers change your life,* she describes her journaling process as:

- A record of my words to God.
- A record of His response to me.
- A way to stay focused.
- A key to avoiding distractions and daydreaming.
- An accountability tool.

- A way of making my appointment with God more like a real meeting.
- An organized way to spend my hour in prayer.
- A systematic way to remember to pray for other people.
- Proof that God answers prayer.
- Eye contact reminding me that this was a two-way conversation.
- A record of my life, my walk, my journey on earth.

Tirabassi writes: "I discovered for myself that prayer was meant to be powerful, give direction, release miracles, bring healing, and offer hope."

Mark Batterson's Journal

Write down the revelation.
—Habakkuk 2:2

A prayer journal can be a valuable tool for developing your relationship with God. The discipline of spending quiet time with the Lord each day can be a life-changing experience. Equip yourself with Bible, journal, and pen.

God speaks to His children. The best way to hear what He is saying is to read the Scriptures daily, praying, "Lord, please speak to me as I read."

When George Muller sensed that God wanted him to establish orphanages for England's needy children, this scripture spoke to him: "Open your mouth wide and I will fill it" (Psalm 81:10). Muller knew that God was telling him to ask for whatever he needed for his orphanage project. In his journal, he wrote a list of things that were needed. Each day he and his wife prayed over the list, and one by one, each item was supplied. The prayer list was not published, and no money was solicited. Eventually, God supplied everything that was needed.

In *Draw the Circle,* Batterson writes: "The same God who helped Muller raise tens of millions of dollars is the same God who can accomplish the plans and purposes which He has put in your heart."

Batterson suggests:

- Read the Bible and ask God to speak to you. When a scripture speaks to your heart, write it in your journal and turn the scripture into a prayer.
- Cry out to God in written prayers. Be honest before God; write about your worries, your fears, your frustrations, or your inability to forgive. When you read the Psalms, you will find that David often expressed his doubts and fears: "*I will say of my God my Rock, "Why have You forgotten me? Why go I mourning because of the oppression of the enemy?"*
- Keep a thanksgiving page, listing your blessings each day, and give thanks to God.
- Keep a prayer list and pray for others.
- Write about your hopes and dreams.
- List baby-steps toward your goals.

In *The Diary of Anne Frank,* we find this inscription:
"I hope I shall be able to confide in you completely, as I have never been able to do in anyone before, and I hope that you will be a great support and comfort." Most of us need someone to confide in, someone to tell our troubles to. Writing letters to God brings support and comfort.

The process of keeping a thanksgiving page will encourage your faith. Find something each day to be thankful for, and express your praise to God, daily.

Talking to God about your hopes and dreams will give focus to your life. God has a unique plan for each of us, and He has supplied us with gifts and abilities to be used in His plan. However, hopes and dreams are nothing more than wishful thoughts if they are not accompanied by definite steps toward those goals. Ask God to show you what steps to take, and list those steps in your journal. Your journal is a private place where you can express your thoughts, feelings, observations, ideas, and convictions.

Flannery O'Connor's Journal

Dear God, tonight it is not disappointing because you have given me a story. Don't let me ever think, dear God, that I was anything but the instrument for Your story.
—Flannery O'Connor

Before Flannery O'Connor became a famous Southern writer, she began keeping a prayer journal. She spelled out her struggles with life and put before the Lord her desires to become a worthy writer. She would write, "I want to succeed in this world, Lord, but I am so discouraged about my work. I am stupid, quite as stupid as the people I ridicule."

She spelled out her sins, expressed her honest doubts, and pleaded to draw closer to the Lord. She would say, "Dear God, I cannot love Thee the way I want to. You are the slim crescent of the moon that I see and my self is the earth's shadow that keeps me from seeing all the moon. I do not know you God because I am in the way. Please help me push myself aside."

Later, she would say, "Oh, dear God, I want to write a novel, a good novel. I want to do this for a good feeling and for a bad one. If I have to sweat for it, Dear God, let it be as in your service. I would like to be intelligently holy. I am a presumptuous fool, but maybe the vague thing in me that keeps me in is hope." Her hope, her honesty before God, and her continual pleadings were rewarded.

The Diary of a Young Girl

I really believe I am a little nutty. My writing's all mixed up. I'm jumping from one thing to another, and sometimes I seriously doubt whether anyone will ever be interested in this drivel. They'll call it "The Musings of an Ugly Duckling." My diaries certainly won't be of much use...

Unless you write yourself, you can't know how wonderful it is. I always used to bemoan the fact that I couldn't draw, but now I am overjoyed that at least I can write. And if I don't have the talent to write books or newspaper articles, I can always write for myself. But I want to achieve more than that... I don't want to live in vain like most people. I want to be useful and bring enjoyment to all people, even those I've never met.

I want to go on living even after my death! And that's why I'm so grateful to God for giving me this gift (of writing), which I can use to develop myself and to express all that's inside me...

When I write I can shake off all my cares, my sorrow disappears, my spirits are revived! The big question is: will I ever be able to write something great?

—Anne Frank, *The Diary of a Young Girl*

Journaling Feelings

Why are you cast down, O my soul? And why are you disquieted within me? Hope in God; for I shall yet praise Him, the help of my countenance and my God.
                    —*Psalm 42:11*

"I am a firm believer in writing down what I am feeling," says Reverend Paula White, "not only as a way of recording my emotions, but also as a way of working out ideas, recording questions, identifying problems, and exploring various issues I desire to bring to resolution. As I read through my old journal, I found certain emotions being expressed repeatedly. I questioned virtually everything in my life. I voiced my pain and sorrow. I struggled to make sense of things that made no sense. I battled a desire to flee far away and yet at the same time, battled a desire to force decisions and resolution. My journal reflected great inner conflict at some points. But as I read on, I also came to pages that revealed other emotions. Things were starting to make sense. I felt more positive. I was filled with love for God and had abounding joy in His presence. I was at peace with those who had hurt me or frustrated me. I was finding answers and solutions.

We need to vent how we feel, or those feelings will build up in us to the point of explosion or decay. We will find ourselves either railing at other people or wallowing in our own bitterness and self-pity. Neither is healthy! Writing your feelings gives them a sense of validity, and that's important. After all, they are your feelings. Find a way of venting what you feel, as you feel it, in a way that works for you and brings you to the point of trusting God wherever you are.

I have been a believer in the principle that if something doesn't kill you, it makes you stronger, and that if you are able to bend just a little and not break, you can ride out just about any storm. It is the presence of God in your life that makes you strong and that defeats the enemy that desires to destroy you. It is God that gives you the enduring strength and flexibility to withstand the severest storm in the darkest of nights. There are seasons in my life when I cry out to God in my journals, expressing both my pain at the circumstances swirling around me and my deep love for God and my joy at His presence."
—Paula White, *You're All That*

My Journal

Trust only in God every moment! Tell Him all your troubles and pour out your heart-longings to Him.
—Psalm 62:8, Passion Bible

My journal is a private place, where proper spelling, punctuation, and sentence structure do not matter. I can confide in my journal, spelling out my thoughts and feelings freely, with no worry of what others may think. These confessions become letters to God; I express my feelings, just as David did in the Psalms. God already knows my thoughts, but as I write about them, I sometimes see myself more clearly. I can talk back to those negative words I've written and then ask God to give me His wisdom for my life.

After I have written about my thoughts and feelings, God speaks to me from the Scriptures. I record those words in my journal. Habakkuk 2:2 says, "Write down the revelation."

I keep a Thanksgiving Page, listing all the blessings of each day. On days when I feel discouraged, I go back to my Thanksgiving Page and give thanks again for each blessing.

Beside my prayer requests, I leave space for the answers as they come. I also list in my journal the things I need to accomplish each month and pray over this list daily. I spell out my hopes and dreams and list the steps I must take to accomplish them. My journal is a written record of my life and my relationship with my heavenly Father.

Inspiring Quotes From My Journal

"Sebastian Bach, spent twenty-seven years at St. Thomas Church in Leipzig, not striving for greatness, but simply getting ready for Sunday. At the head of many of his compositions he wrote the Latin initials for 'Jesus Help,' and at the end, 'To God Alone Be Glory.'"
—Michael Card, *Scribbling in the Sand*

"There are moments when God has touched our lives like a soft hand of morning sun reaching in through our bedroom window… It may be a word telling us who we are and why we are here and what is required of us at this particular juncture of our journey."
-Ken Gire, *Windows of the Soul*

"Pray to catch the bus, then run as fast as you can."
–Julia Cameron

"Prayer is not a substitute for work, or merely a preparation for work. It is work."
-Ronald Dunn

"God guides our minds as we think things out in His presence."
–J.I. Packer

"Praying on sleepless nights—thank goodness, God knows all this stuff and is gracious enough to let me in on how it all works, though I must tell you He hardly ever gives me the big picture. I only get a little insight at a time. In the same way the beam of flashlight, on a

very dark night, gives just enough illumination for one step at a time. Step into the beam of light."
–Jan Karon, *At Home in Mitford*

"If the blind put their hand in God's they find their way more surely than those who see but have no faith or purpose."
–Helen Keller

"Earth's crammed with heaven, and every common bush afire with God; but only he who sees takes off his shoes; the rest sit round it and pluck blackberries."
—Elizabeth Barrett Browning

Chapter Seven

Giving Thanks

In everything give thanks; for this is the will of God in Christ Jesus for you.
—*1 Thessalonians 5:18*

Choosing to Give Thanks

You have turned for me my mourning into dancing; You have put off my sackcloth and clothed me with gladness, to the end that my glory may sing praise to You and not be silent. O Lord my God, I will give thanks to You forever.
-*Psalm 30:11-12*

Paging through author Nancy DeMoss's book, *Choosing Gratitude*, I began reading a heart-rending story which took place in India: A three-year-old boy is leaning against the cot of his dying mother. The boy's eyes are hollow, his stomach distended, and his face is fly-infested. "Standing there in that slum," says missionary Paul Tripp, "I felt all complaints I had ever spoken as if they were a weight on my shoulders."

Later, when Tripp returned to his home in America, he asked a church leader from India who had come to the states to study, "What do you think of Americans?" The man from India answered, "You have no idea how much you have, and yet you always complain."

As I read this story, I am humbled and ashamed of my self-centered grumbling. I am nudged to give thanks for "common mercies," such as bath soap, toothpaste, hot water, air-conditioning, and so many other comforts. I also give thanks for the great big things: Excellent medical care, kind, caring people who treat me with dignity in my most vulnerable moments, books that elevate my thoughts, and prayers that others pray for me.

DeMoss also brings up the matter of giving thanks to God for those who have touched our lives and who need our expressed gratitude. As an example, she writes about Pastor William Stidger, who wrote a letter of thanks to his English teacher who had first inspired in him a love for literature and poetry. Later, Stidger received a note from his former teacher: "William, I can't tell you how much your note meant to me. I am in my eighties, living alone in a small room, lonely, like the last leaf of autumn lingering behind. I taught in school for more than fifty years, and yours is the first note of appreciation I have ever received. It came on a blue, cold morning, and it cheered me as nothing has done in many years."

My husband, a retired Air Traffic Controller, believes it is important to say thank you to mentors. He wrote a letter to someone who touched his life many years ago: "Colonel Sam, you had a great influence on me when I was a young man. Because I was underweight, I had failed the physical required for entering Air Traffic Control School. You flew me to Keesler Air Force Base in the summer of 1954 for a second physical. Perhaps you thought I was still too skinny to pass. When we were airborne, you handed me a sack of bananas and said, 'Eat these and you will weigh more.' I ate the bananas and passed the physical, and that opened the door to my future." Later, Colonel Sam Forbert, who is now in his nineties, responded with a phone call, telling my husband how much he appreciated the letter of thanks.

Saying Grace

It is customary in most households, where the family spirit recognizes the kindness of God in guarding the lives and souls of his people, to pause for a moment before the meal at which the family is gathered together and have offered a simple prayer of thanks to the Father in heaven for his provision of the means by which we live. This act of devotion, simple as it may appear, doubtless has kept pure and holy the spirits of untold millions, to who its observance is both an act of sincere gratitude and a gentle but powerful reminder of the constant relation between our Lord and His children. —Grace Before Meals, 1911

Ask any native of Savannah, Georgia where to eat lunch, and one of the first suggestions you will hear is Mrs. Wilkes' restaurant on Jones Street. The old boarding house is a landmark in the middle of a charming nostalgic city. It nestles underneath ancient live oaks, alongside a vintage brick-paved street. If you get there before eleven O'clock on a weekday morning, you will find tourists and local folks in a long waiting line, scrawling down Jones Street. At eleven o'clock sharp, the door opens to the historical Brownstone, and lots of hungry people file in.

My friend from Savannah, Keith Howington, once took me to this restaurant. Big, round tables were spread with platters of crispy fried chicken, ham, bowls of beef-stew, creamed potatoes and gravy, collard greens, squash, black-eyed peas, fried okra, cornbread, and numerous other southern delights. As we made our way to one of the tables, Keith instructed, "No one eats until Mrs. Wilkes comes. Then, we hold hands we will hold hands around our table while she says the blessing over the food." It has been several years since my visit to Savannah. The last time I spoke with Keith, he told me that even though Mrs. Wilkes had passed away, the old tradition of "Grace before meals" was still taking place in the heart of a very sophisticated city.

In Sevierville, Tennessee, several years ago, Jim and Lill Katzbeck carried on the same tradition in their charming Bed and Breakfast, located on top of a tranquil mountain. Each morning, when the aroma of freshly brewed coffee filled the air, a long pine table was laid with hot biscuits, crispy bacon and sausage, eggs, grits, pastries, fruit, and homemade jelly. Jim and Lill invited their guests to hold hands around the table while Lill asked God's blessing upon the food. In her prayer she said, "And please, Lord, provide for those who have no food today."

The last time we ate at Peggy's Restaurant in Philadelphia, Mississippi, we served ourselves and sat at a boarding-house style table. As I glanced across the room to another table, I saw a black man extending his hand toward the white man across the table, and together, they asked God's blessing upon their food.

Once, in a local restaurant, my husband and I bowed our heads for a quick blessing. Just as we concluded the prayer, another voice joined us with a rousing "Amen!" We looked up to find our waitress standing beside the table. This opened a conversation about faith in which the young woman began telling us about her prayer needs.

I believe that the practice of joining hands around the table in honor of God is a true picture of the heart of America. It gives me comfort to believe that in the midst of the mindless, and often godless, sophistication of cities and towns across the land, there remains a core group of believers who continually offer up simple prayers of thanksgiving to our Father in Heaven for His provision of the means by which we live.

Pizza, Pasta, & Prayer

When God sees a problem, He puts people on earth to fix it. And what each of us needs to do is to remember what we're here for.
  —Guideposts Magazine

It was mealtime, but there was very little food in the Oleson household. The last bit of food, one apple and a carrot, would not make a meal for six people. Nevertheless, the mother would set the table, slice the apple, and place it on the table. And then, the family would sit down and give thanks for what they had.

Across town, at Little Joe's Pizza, the Brasmer family members were celebrating a birthday. Faith and Bob, along with their daughters Debbie and Jeanne, were served large portions of pasta and pizza. When they had eaten all they could possibly eat, they asked for a carryout container.

Leaving the restaurant with a large box of food, they discussed among themselves what could be done with the leftovers. When they drove into the neighborhood, into their neighborhood, the thought came to Faith that the children next door might enjoy some pizza. Minutes later, having no idea how hungry their neighbors were, the Brasmers found themselves delivering pizza and pasta to the Oleson family. After surprised greetings, the two families rejoiced that God had honored thanksgiving prayers from the needy ones and nudged those who had more than enough to share their blessings.

A similar story is told in Debbie Macomber's book, *One Perfect Word*: A young seminary student and his wife were barely getting by, with bills to be paid and very little money. Their food supply was short, and they began eating oatmeal three times a day. With nothing in the cupboard but oatmeal, they received news that an old friend would be stopping by for dinner the next evening. The wife exclaimed, "We can't feed them oatmeal for dinner! What are we going to do?"

For a moment the husband was speechless, and then he said, "We've been studying in seminary class about what to do in impossible situations, the first thing we're supposed to do is pray."

So, they bowed their heads and the husband prayed, "Lord, we don't have any food to serve our friend, so we ask You to provide a good meal for our friend when he comes tomorrow."

After the prayer, the husband asked his wife: "Let's think about what we would serve for dinner tomorrow night if we had plenty of money."

The young wife smiled and said, "I have Mamma's meatloaf recipe. I'd cook that."

"Meatloaf, what would you need for that?" asked her husband. He reached for a pencil and began writing a grocery list, as his wife called out the ingredients.

She said, "I'd start with two pounds of hamburger, and I would need onion and eggs. And if we could have catsup on top, that would look pretty. We would need potatoes for baking and sour cream and butter, and green beans." And then she said, "I wish we had Kentucky Wonder beans, and it would be great to have strawberries and cream for dessert, and we would need coffee to go with it."

The husband placed his hand on the completed list and prayed, "Lord, here's what we're asking You to provide for tomorrow's dinner. We don't know how you're going to do this, but we trust You and thank You. Amen!" In faith, the wife set the table for the next night's dinner.

When the husband returned from classes the next afternoon, delicious smells greeted him. He peeped into the oven and found a meatloaf and three large baking potatoes. The wife began telling what had happened: She had heard a knock at the door, but when she opened the door nobody was there, just a box filled with food. They had a lovely dinner that night with their friend.

Eventually, the young husband graduated, became a pastor, and then took on the role of a traveling evangelist. One of his trips took him back to the town where the seminary was located. As he spoke one night at a local church, he told the story of God's miraculous dinner provision of some years back. An elderly lady greeted him after the service and said, "Thank you for telling about the meatloaf, because you have cleared up something I've wondered about for years." And she began telling her story:

> "My husband and I owned the little grocery store where you and your wife used to buy oatmeal. You never bought anything but oatmeal. We wanted to help you, but every time we prayed about you, it was just as though the Lord was saying, 'not yet.' Then one morning I knew the Lord was saying, 'Today's the day!' Well I couldn't wait to get to the store. Fresh vegetables had just arrived that morning, so I grabbed a box and picked up two of the largest baking potatoes I'd ever seen. And the Lord said, 'Get three potatoes.' So, I put the third potato in the box and added butter and sour cream. Then I placed three handfuls of the prettiest long green beans in the box—I think they were called Kentucky Wonders. And I just knew I was supposed to include the beautiful seasonal strawberries, cream too, and coffee. When I went over to the meat case, I began pulling out large steaks. But the Lord said, 'No.' I touched a roast and heard within my spirit the same 'No,' I touched the pork chops and heard 'No' again. Finally, I put my hand on the hamburger meat, the Lord said, 'Two pounds.'"

Faith, thanksgiving, and praise opens doors for God to meet our needs.

Chapter Eight

Praying For Our Nation

The Moravians prayed, and the greatest revival of that time hit the world. Finney prayed—America rocked with power. Hudson Taylor prayed, and China's inland mission was born. Evans Roberts prayed seven years, until the Welsh revival resulted. An old Negro, Seymore of Azusa, prayed for five hours a day for three and a half years. He prayed seven hours a day for one and a half more years and Heaven's Fire fell over the world, the most extensive revival of real religion in the century resulted. America has grown in numbers, wealth, and power as no other nation has ever grown... We have vainly imagined, in the deceitfulness of our hearts, that all these blessings were produced by some superior wisdom and virtue of our own... We have become too proud to pray to the God that made us!
—Derek Prince

THE REMNANT

If My people who are called by My name will humble themselves, and pray and seek My face, and turn from

> *their wicked ways, then I will hear from heaven, and will forgive their sin and heal their land.*
> —2 Chronicles 7:14

In the novel *Thunder from Jerusalem*, written by Christian authors Brock and Bodie Thoene, there is a story illustrating the responsibility of "God's people" in our world today. One of the main characters in the book, Grandfather, a Jewish Rabbi, says to his granddaughter, "*The Lamedvov. The thirty-six righteous ones. Do you understand what I am saying, Rachel?*"

"*Papa used to speak of it,*" say Rachel. "*A famous legend.*"

"*No Legend,*" says Grandfather. "*Lamedvov. Thirty-six righteous souls who live upon the earth in each generation. It is the Lamedvov who hold back God's judgment on the world. The Lamedvov may be man or woman, Jew or Gentile. Together they are the true remnant of righteousness.*"

The story of the *Lamedvov* is based in part on the story of Abraham and his conversation with the Lord about the destruction of Sodom in Genesis—those who, by virtue of their compassion for others and the prayers they offer, causes the Lord to answer, "I will spare the whole place for their sakes" (Genesis 18:26).

The *Lamedvov* are humble servants of their fellows, tirelessly working to dry tears, show compassion, and shoulder the burden of those who suffer. The Thirty-Six have felt the Shechinah, the Divine Presence. They have recognized the power of God in their lives—the pillows of cloud and the fire—which guides them and protects them. The Lamedvov are not powerless in this wicked world. Rather, they use the gifts and talents which they possess to lift all those around them. They help to save us all. Will He spare the whole place for their sakes?

I believe the Thirty-Six have multiplied into throngs of humble servants who believe the Word of God. They humble themselves daily; they pray and seek God's face. They turn from their wicked ways. They cry out, and claim His promise to heal our land.

Dear Lord, show us how to be Your remnant of righteousness in our world today. By our prayers, help us to tip the balance of a suffering world on the brink of collapse.

SHAPING HISTORY THROUGH PRAYER

Then the Lord saw it, and it displeased Him that there was no justice. He saw that there was no man, and wondered that there was no intercessor.
—Isaiah 59:15-16

American history has often been shaped by prayer. Before the Pilgrims knelt on the dock at Delftshaven, asking for God's blessing on their journey to the "Promised Land," a day of fasting and prayer was declared to prepare them for the arduous voyage.

In *Plymouth Plantation,* author/historian William Bradford described the scene as the Pilgrims entered America: "Being thus arrived in a good harbor and brought safe to land, they fell upon their knees and blessed the God of heaven who had brought them over the vast and furious ocean, and delivered them from all the perils and miseries thereof…"

In the summer of 1623, the corn crop which the Pilgrims had planted was threatened. Concerning this, Bradford wrote: "By a great drought which continued from the third week of May, until about the middle of July, without any rain, the corn began to dwindle away. Upon which they set apart a solemn day of humiliation to seek the Lord by humble and fervent prayer. And He was pleased to give them a gracious and speedy answer with such sweet and gentle showers as gave them cause of rejoicing and blessing God. It came without either wind or thunder. The earth was thoroughly soaked there with."

This practice of setting aside special days of prayer and fasting became an accepted part of life on Plymouth Plantation.

In Derek Prince's book, *Shaping History Through Prayer*, he stated that when the British Parliament ordered an embargo on the Port of Boston, Massachusetts in 1774, the Burgesses of Virginia immediately passed a resolution protesting this act and set aside June 1 as a day of fasting and prayer. Consequently, George Washington wrote in his diary on June 1, 1774: *"WE went to church and fasted all day."* John Adams, James Madison, and Abraham Lincoln also proclaimed days of fasting and prayer during their presidencies.

Similarly, Benjamin Franklin's plea at the Constitutional Convention of 1787 has a message for America has a message for America in our present time: "In the beginning of the contest with Britain, when we were sensible of danger, we had daily prayers in the room for Divine protection. Our prayers Sir, were heard, and they were graciously answered. All of us who were engaged in the struggle must have observed frequent instances of a superintending Providence. And have we now forgotten this Powerful Friend? Or do we imagine we no longer need His assistance? The longer I live, the more convincing proofs I see of this truth. 'God governs in the affairs of man.' And if a sparrow cannot fall to the ground without His notice, is it probable that an empire can rise without His aid? I therefore beg leave to move that, henceforth, prayers imploring the assistance of Heaven and its blessing on our deliberation be held."

The Hardest Thing

Prayer is the hardest thing. And no one congratulates you for doing it because no one knows you're doing it, and if things turn out well, they likely won't thank God in any case. But I have a feeling that the hardest thing is what we all better be doing now, and that it's not only the best answer but the only one.

—Peggy Noonan, *Wall Street Journal*

The alarm clock jolted me out of a peaceful sleep. I struggled up, trying to remember why I had set the alarm. As my sleepy brain slowly focused, I recalled signing the prayer chart at church on Sunday night, agreeing to pray every morning for our America. It was a chilly morning, and the bed was warm and cozy. I thought maybe I could stay in bed and pray. I sat up, propped myself will pillows, pulled the warm quilt up to my neck, and began, "Dear God..."

I woke sometime later with a start. This was not working; maybe I should get out of bed and get on my knees. I pulled on my robe, sank to my knees in front of my favorite chair, and began once more, "Dear God..."

I nodded off again, and when I woke, I remembered the scene at Gethsemane on the night before Jesus was crucified. He said to his disciples: "Can you not wait with me and pray one hour?" When the Son of God needed the prayers of his disciples, they were too sleepy to pray. Just as Jesus needed his disciples to wake up and pray, God needs His people in America to awaken and intercede for their country.

WHAT DOES GOD DESIRE FOR AMERICA?

> *How many things the Lord indeed desires to do, yet He does not perform them because His people do not pray. He will wait until men agree with Him, and then He will work. This is a great principle in God's working, and it constitutes one of the most important principles to be found in the Bible.*
> —Watchman Nee

The United States of America was born through the efforts of earnest prayer, and prayer has always been the answer for its problems. When a financial panic hit our country in 1857, more than thirty thousand men wandered the streets of New York City, jobless, and in despair. Jeremiah Lamphier, a quiet business man, took pity on these men and began praying for them. He sent out twenty thousand flyers announcing a noonday prayer meeting. In the beginning, only five men joined him. But the word spread, and within weeks, great numbers of men responded. Eventually, because of the New York prayer meetings, similar groups sprang up around the nation. It is estimated that one million people across the nation were touched by these prayers, and conditions began to change.

In 1987, Ronald Reagan said, "Mr. Gorbachev, tear down this wall!" Two years later the Berlin Wall crumbled, bringing peace to Germany. This victory began with a prayer meeting. Six people in a prayer group met each Monday night at St. Nicholas Church in Leipzig, Germany. This evolved into thousands of people across East and West Germany praying for peace. People interceded in homes, churches, and the streets. These prayers brought the Berlin Wall down.

In the late Seventies, America's economy was failing, with inflation, unemployment, and long gas lines. American embassies around the world were under attack, and Iranians were shouting, "Death to America!" while Americans were being held hostage in Iran, and an attempt to rescue them failed, a prayer meeting was organized, called Washington for Jesus.

In 1980, taking as their theme 2 Chronicles 7:14, people from all over the country met in Washington. They lifted their hands toward the steps of the capitol and prayed that God would bring men and women into the government who would do God's will. They prayed that the hostages in Iran would be released. In 1981, on Inauguration Day, as Ronald Reagan was being sworn in, word came that the American hostages had been released.

Let's do the hardest thing: Let's wake up and pray!

Notes

CHAPTER TWO – HOW TO PRAY

Batterson, Mark, *The Circle Maker*. Grand Rapids, Michigan, Zondervan, 2011.

Keller, Timothy, *Prayer: Experiencing Awe and Intimacy with God*. New York, New York: Penguin Group, 2014.

L'Engle, Madeleine, *Walking on Water*. Colorado Springs, Co. Waterbrook Press, 2006.

Macomber, Debbie, *One Perfect Word. New York, N.Y.: Howard Books, 2012.*

Malz, Betty, *Prayers that are Answered*. New York, New York: Signet, 1981.

Miller, Basil, *George Muller: Man of faith and miracles: Minneapolis, Minnesota:* Bethany House Publishers

Peale, Norman Vincent, *Power of Positive Thinking*. New York, N.Y.: Simon & Shuster, 1952.

Sheets, Dutch, *Intercessory Prayer*. Ventura, California: Regal, 1996.

Spurgeon, Charles, *The Power of Prayer in a Believer's Life*. Lynnwood, Washington: Emerald Books, 1993.

Vella, Christina, *George Washington Carver*. Louisiana University Press, 2015.

Wilkinson, Bruce, *The Prayer of Jabez*, Sisters, Oregon: Multnomah Publishers, 2000.

Chapter Three – Life Saving Prayers

Jordan, River, *Praying for Strangers*. New York, New York: Berkley Books, 2011.

Lake, Alexander, *Your Prayers are Always Answered*. New York, New York: Simon & Schuster, 1956.

Chapter Four – Prayers That Never Die

Carson, Ben, *Gifted Hands*. Grand Rapids, Michigan: Zondervan, 1990.

Graham, Ruth Bell, *Prodigals and Those Who Love Them*. Colorado Springs,

Colorado: Focus on the Family, 1991.

Marshall, Catherine, *Beyond Ourselves*. New York, New York: Avon Books, 1961.

Osteen, Joel, *Break Out*. New York, New York: Faith Words, 2013.

Chapter Five – Impossible Things

Burpo, Todd, *Heaven is for Real,* Nashville, Tennessee: Thomas Nelson, 2010.

Cymbala, Jim, *Breakthrough Prayer,* Grand Rapids, Michigan: Zondervan Publishing, 2003.

Cymbala, Jim, *Fresh Wind Fresh Fire,* Grand Rapids Michigan, Zondervan Publishing, 1997.

Neal, Mary C., *To Heaven and Back,* Colorado Springs, Colorado: Waterbrook Press, 2011.

Nee, Watchman, *Let Us Pray,* New York, New York: Christian Fellowship Publishers, 1977.

Chapter Six – Journaling

Batterson, Mark, *Draw the Circle,* Grand Rapids, Michigan: Zondervan, 2012.

Frank, Anne, The Diary of a Young Girl, New York, New York: Pocket Books, 1958.

O'Connor, Flannery, *A Prayer Journal,* New York, N.Y.: Farrar, Straus, & Giroux, 2013.

Tirabassi, Becky, *Change Your Life, New York, New York:* G.P. Putnam Sons, 2000.

White, Paula, *You're All That,* New York, New York: Hachette Book Group, 2007.

Chapter Eight – Praying for Our Nation

Prince, Derek, *Shaping History Through Prayer and Fasting,* New Kensington, Pa: Whitaker House 1973.

Thoene, Bodie, *Thunder from Jerusalem,* New York, N.Y.: Viking, 2000.

Ingram Content Group UK Ltd.
Milton Keynes UK
UKHW042017090323
418309UK00001B/60